What peopl

Ba

*Bag Lady* is a great read for someone starting a business with a purpose. The book contains interesting personal anecdotes, sound business advice and leaves readers with useful knowledge and enhanced confidence to step out on their own in a meaningful pursuit.

**Kenneth Cole**, Designer and Social Activist

If you want to make a difference in the world but aren't sure how, grab this insightful book. From the first eye-opening pages about the harms of plastic bags, to inspiring stories about finding the confidence to build a climate-friendly business, *Bag Lady* is a compelling read. With charm and candor, Lisa Foster spells out the important personal and business lessons that helped her overcome impossible odds and succeed.

**Rosabeth Moss Kanter**, Harvard Business School professor and award-winning author of *Confidence* and *Think Outside the Building*

Today, there is endless opportunity to join the movement for sustainability, and *Bag Lady* shows you the way! The story of one woman's quest to do good leads her in an unforeseen direction that eventually kickstarts a movement! Read how an eye-opening moment of clarity was marshalled into a passion that ultimately made a huge difference on our climate crisis and our plastic pollution problem.

**Laurie David**, producer of *An Inconvenient Truth*, environmental advocate, and author of *Imagine It: A Handbook for a Happier Planet*

*Bag Lady* is an inspiring read that makes you want to find out what happens next. Lisa Foster offers a compelling personal

exploration of imagination, growth, hardship, and triumph that will resonate with every entrepreneur. More importantly, she demonstrates how a social entrepreneur who commits to a larger purpose can literally change our world for the better.
**Tom Bowman**, founder of Bowman Change, Inc., and author of *What If Solving the Climate Crisis Is Simple?*

Lisa Foster's book *Bag Lady* is a master class for all who wish to make a difference in the world. As she recounts her journey from English teacher to eco-entrepreneur, the reader will be inspired by her courage, persistence, and values—all necessary to the process of positive change. Readers will also get an instructive look at the management skills one has to master to successfully grow an enterprise. And finally, Lisa's honest account of successes, setbacks and lessons learned are invaluable gifts to guide all who seek change, whether it be in building a business or transitioning a life. This story is both timely and essential as the world awakens to the transformational benefits female-owned businesses offer society.
**Bob Rosenberg**, 35-year CEO of Dunkin' Donuts and author of *Around the Corner to Around the World*

You must read this book. It takes you on the remarkable journey of an amazing eco-entrepreneur who's committed to changing the way we shop. The valuable and practical tools and tips Lisa Foster shares will help any business leader launch and run a business that's committed to making the world a better place.
**Jeffrey Hollender**, co-founder and CEO, American Sustainable Business Network; co-founder and former CEO, Seventh Generation; Adjunct Professor, Stern School of Business

Written with warmth and verve, *Bag Lady* is a marvelous tribute to entrepreneurship's power to change the world. In telling the story of 1 Bag at a Time, Lisa Foster shows the gift, so rare among business leaders, of conveying wisdom without platitudes and guidance without jargon. This is a book to inspire innovators and idealists alike.

**Joseph E. Aoun**, President, Northeastern University

Cheers to *Bag Lady*! It is a clear and poetic testament to what one person can do, and it is also a very clear and prosaic testament to the glories and challenges of starting a business. Following the simple idea that one person can change the world, Lisa started 1 Bag at a Time. As a result, my grandchildren will not have to see nearly as many plastic bags wrapped around fences, drifting into the ocean, slowly decomposing into the dangerous molecules of plastic that are so toxic to our world. This book is resonant with Lisa's pride in her progress and with her scrupulous self-admissions of her failures. It will be inspiring to anyone who has an idea for a business and even more so if that idea has a goal within it of leaving this world a better place. And that is, without a doubt, exactly what Lisa Foster has done.

**Mary Steenburgen**, American actress, comedian, singer, and songwriter

# Bag Lady

How I Started a Business for a
Greener World and Changed
the Way America Shops

# Bag Lady

## How I Started a Business for a Greener World and Changed the Way America Shops

Lisa D. Foster

CHANGEMAKERS
BOOKS

Winchester, UK
Washington, USA

JOHN HUNT PUBLISHING

First published by Changemakers Books, 2022
Changemakers Books is an imprint of John Hunt Publishing Ltd., No. 3 East Street,
Alresford, Hampshire SO24 9EE, UK
office@jhpbooks.com
www.johnhuntpublishing.com
www.changemakers-books.com

For distributor details and how to order please visit the 'Ordering' section on our website.

ISBN: 978 1 80341 166 8
978 1 80341 167 5 978 1 80341 166 8 (ebook)
Library of Congress Control Number: 2021952711

Design: Matthew Greenfield


UK: Printed and bound by CPI Group (UK) Ltd, Croydon, CR0 4YY
Printed in North America by CPI GPS partners

We operate a distinctive and ethical publishing philosophy in
all areas of our business, from our global network of authors to
production and worldwide distribution.

# Contents

*For Gary, Daryn, and Kayla—always.*

*Just do one thing.*

# Acknowledgements

I know it's customary to put your family last, but Gary, Daryn, and Kayla are always first for me. Alex, you too. Your belief in me has empowered me to go far beyond where I thought I could go. Many thanks to my entire UpIsland Book Group who were the first to encourage me to dream my impossible dream: Rosabeth Moss Kanter, Cheryl Batzer, Joanne Ashe, Donna Weisman, Mary Steenburgen, Leone Webster, Gerri Sweder, Nina Fialkow, and everyone else who cheered me on and urged me to take the first leap.

I would not be where I am without the support of my many friends from Martha's Vineyard, including Laurie David who told me powerfully to just do one thing, Michael Norkus who showed me how to start, Linda Koren who was an early customer, Bob Rosenberg who made me feel like a pro, Bill Hake who helped me with business planning, Steve Bernier who took a chance on me when I was starting out, Simon Shapiro who introduced me to Ace, and the mystery customer who sent my bags across the US in 2007 and started a trend in cities far and wide. Thanks too *in memoriam* to Guy Webster whose beautiful photos helped my customers envision the beauty of a reusable lifestyle.

I owe a lot of my success to the many people who encouraged me along the way: Jeffrey Hollender who first sponsored a badge for me at Expo West and later introduced me to Verité, Tom Hudnut who introduced me to Ralph's, Karly Katona who took up the cause of reusable bags at LA County, David Fialkow who was always ready to connect me to anyone who could be of help, and many people from Northeastern University who championed my achievements and empowered me, including Patty Flint, Tami Baringer, Diane MacGillivray, and Joseph Aoun.

I'm deeply grateful for Amy Li Ping and John Lovell, my international teammates and friends, who supported my vision for an ethically sourced, quality bag and built an incredible team of people who made it happen. Thanks, too, to Char Krasnoff, and to Tony Fu who served as my international supply expert, mentor, and friend, and to everyone who worked on my team in LA.

Many thanks also to Tim Ward at John Hunt Publishing for seeing the potential in my story, encouraging me as a writer, and helping me spread my message.

To every Chinese factory worker who made my products and every US customer who bought a bag from 1 Bag at a Time—thank you. You're the reason I woke up every day for 12 years and went to work.

# Introduction

# Would You Like a Bag?

Not long ago, I went to the grocery store to pick up a couple of items. At checkout, the cashier asked, Would you like a bag?

This may sound like a completely unremarkable incident, but not for me. Not long ago, the only question a cashier asked was: Paper or plastic? Often, they didn't even ask. If I purchased even one item—an apple, say, or a pack of gum—they would bag it in plastic before I could say a word.

This book is about how I transformed myself from high-school English teacher to eco-entrepreneur in order to change the question at grocery stores across America from *Paper or plastic?* to *Would you like a bag?* When I discovered reusable bags on a trip to Australia in 2005, I became obsessed. Getting Americans to change the way we shop by switching to reusable bags became, for me, a moral imperative. It was personal. I had no idea how to do it. I just knew I had to.

I was far from sure that I would succeed. Nine out of ten startups fail. I had no training or background in business, so the odds were even worse for me. Also, a market for reusable bags in the US didn't exist. Friends told me not to do it, that Americans would never bring their bags back to the store. But I was determined. Australia and Ireland had already gone reusable. I believed deeply in my heart that America could do the same, creating significant reductions in plastic waste and global emissions. If I could be the one helping people make that switch, it would be worth whatever it took.

So, I set out to transform myself into the Bag Lady, an entrepreneur on a mission to save the world one bag at a time. I wasn't sure I would make any money, but I promised not to lose any, at least not much. It wasn't about money. It was about listening to my heart and dedicating myself to a larger purpose, and that turned out to be a combination that drove a lot of success. Not only did I inspire millions of Americans to switch to reusable bags, I helped ignite a movement against single-use plastics that continues to reduce plastic waste today.

I didn't know it then, but as I set out to change the world one bag at a time, other business leaders had begun to see the power of aligning business interests with environmental and social interests on a much larger scale. Of course, most people, if they have to choose between going broke or breaking the world, will choose not to go broke. But my experience, and that of others, shows the choice is a false one. Over the last few decades, many businesses are finding ways to put people and the planet on the same side of the equation as profit.[1]

It takes vision, innovation, and courage, and it's happening. Many businesses are changing their business models to become more sustainable and equitable. Purpose-driven companies are transforming waste and energy sectors. Giant retail companies are finding that sustainability initiatives increase their profit and market share, like Unilever's sustainable tea initiative, Walmart's commitment to an all-electric transportation fleet, and Aetna Insurance's decision to raise its minimum wage to $16 an hour. More are following. When you start to price in the cost in terms of human health and extreme climate events, the business case starts to make sense. Rarely has innovation, technology, and social will all aligned so powerfully as now to create the possibility for so much positive change.

If you have ever wanted to make a difference in the world, I hope my book will inspire you to act on your passions. You know the problems that light a fire in your heart, the problems that need to be solved now to create a better world for ourselves and our future. You don't need any special education or knowledge to start. All you need is a desire to make a positive impact on an issue and a willingness to learn the rest.

Don't worry if the problem you want to solve seems small. You can't expect to solve everything. Just do one thing. If we all did just one thing, together we could create the world we want to live in. The little things we do every day, like reusing a bag, add up to the big changes we need for a better future.

## Chapter 1

# The Tragic Life of a Plastic Bag

Plastic bags are among the most ubiquitous items on earth. The Environmental Protection Agency (EPA) estimates that the US alone uses about 380 billion bags or sacks a year. That's more than a billion bags a day. It happens one consumer and one bag at a time.

So, what happens when you throw a bag away? It's easy to forget about it and think that's the end. The reality is a lot more complicated.

> *When you throw a bag away, there is no away. There is only here.*

All the plastic ever produced is still somewhere here on earth. When you throw a bag away, there is no away. There is only here.

At best, once you have used them, plastic bags end up in landfill where we will have to maintain them for thousands of years. Landfills are essentially large pits lined with concrete where we put all the things that we don't want to put back in our environment. Plastic bags are not diverted to recycling centers because they tend to jam recycling machinery. Less than 5% of plastic bags[2] end up in recycling anyway.

Unfortunately, the vast majority of plastic bags aren't recycled. About a third of them, actually 32% of the billion bags we use every day, never make it to landfill.[3] Some are simply littered—thrown out of car windows or ditched on urban streets. Most, of course, are responsibly thrown into a trash bin somewhere, but that doesn't mean they stay there. They frequently blow right out of public trash bins, few of which have lids to keep them inside. Even if you put a plastic bag in a trash can at home, you can't assume it will arrive safely at a landfill. It can blow out onto the street when the trash can is on the curb or when the trash truck empties your trash can into its belly. They even blow out of trash trucks while on the road, or out of landfills if they get there.

Once they are in the environment, plastic bags blow around, sometimes sticking in trees or onto electrical wires. As you go about your daily business, you have probably seen them wafting over the roadways or clogging street gutters. Out in the environment, they eventually break up into smaller pieces, falling to the ground. When it rains, they wash into gutters, streams, and waterways, just as the rains have been washing debris into our waters for millennia. There, through exposure to sun and currents, they break up into even smaller pieces, and finally, these little bits of plastic wash into the ocean.

Ocean currents swirl around against continental shores like a gigantic toilet bowl, but there's no flush. If you put a rubber ducky on a shore anywhere, it would theoretically take 12 years for the currents to swirl it in ever smaller circles until it reached the center of the ocean, or what marine scientists call the gyre. Until the advent of plastic in the early 1900s, everything caught in ocean currents was biodegradable and would break down into organic matter before it reached the center of the ocean, so the water there was pristine. But in the last century or so, the plastic that found its way into ocean currents began to build up in the gyres, farthest from land. Charles Moore famously discovered what he called The Great Pacific Garbage Patch in 1997 in the north Pacific Gyre. It's not really a floating island of plastic, as many people imagine. It's more like a cloudy concentration of plastic bits, more or less mixed with water, sloshing around. Much of the plastic is thought to sink below it, creating a heap of plastic trash at the bottom of the center of the ocean.

About 54% of the plastic in the gyre is estimated to come from land-based activities: dropped water bottles, broken Styrofoam cups, and of course, plastic shopping bags. The rest comes from boats, commercial and private, and from shipping containers.[4]

Altogether, the equivalent of a city garbage truck's worth of plastic is dumped into the ocean every minute,[5] amounting to 8 million metric tons annually.[6] Governments spend an estimated $40 billion a year in cleanup costs.[7]

That is why free bags are not really free. The billions of dollars local governments pay for cleanup is ultimately funded by our tax dollars. The Department of the Environment in San Francisco estimated that each bag cost the city 17 cents in disposal and cleanup costs. And it's not just our tax dollars that are inflated by so-called free plastic bags. Plastic bags in the US in 2005 were an estimated $4-billion-dollar-a-year industry, consuming some 12 million barrels of petroleum annually. Still today, many stores hand out bags to consumers free of charge and pass billions of dollars in purchasing costs on to consumers as overhead, effectively hiding the cost of plastic bags in other items like milk and light bulbs. Ultimately, consumers and citizens bear all these costs, whether we are aware of it or not.

Of course, all the plastic that we can't clean up finds its way to our oceans where it is interfering with marine life. Plastic bottle caps and other items that tend to float attract marine birds like the albatross, which can go years without touching land. Photos by Chris Jordan on Midway Atoll,[8] a small island not far from Hawaii and one of the nearest land areas to the Pacific Gyre, show haunting skeletons of albatross chicks decomposing with stomachs full of plastic, unable to eat and digest their normal foods. Sea turtles have been found with plastic straws in their noses or six-pack rings around their necks. Over 700 species of animals and fish have been found with plastic bags inside their bellies or tangled up outside of them.[9]

Plastic poses dangers far beyond entanglement, dangers we can't see or photograph, from the endocrine-disrupting compounds they are made with, like BPA and other chemicals. Exposure to these chemicals interferes with the reproductive cycle of animals, including orca whales,[10] Arctic seals, polar bears, and many others.[11] Toxins concentrate as they move up the food chain, so evidence of infertility and hormonal irregularities in large animals indicates toxic effects throughout a wide variety of species.

An increasing incidence of intersex or ambiguous sexual variation among people has also been observed. These gender abnormalities have been tied to exposure *in utero* to the endocrine-disrupting chemicals from plastic.[12] Besides the ubiquitous plastic food-containers that much of our food supply depends on, some of which may be leaching chemicals into what we eat, studies have found microplastic bits in a number of common foods, including of course fish, but also table salt, beer, bottled water, and even tap water. Scientists have calculated that for men in Western countries, sperm count has declined 59% from 1973 to 2011, much of that due to exposure to endocrine-disrupting chemicals in plastic.[13]

We may think we're throwing plastic away, but there is no away. It is coming back to us on our plates. It's reaching into our wallets and into our bodies.

**Chapter 2**

# If You're Going to Be Something, Be the Best

I learned the facts about plastic bags and wrote The Tragic Life of a Plastic Bag after a trip to Australia. It was a six-month, through-the-looking-glass trip, and coming back, I would not be the same.

When I first arrived in Melbourne on January 2, 2005, my first impression was how hot it was. It didn't seem like the same sun that shined on us in the US but a much hotter version. Scorching. That was the day I first heard the question that would change my life: Would you like a bag?

It would take me a while to sort out why the sun was hotter there and why nearly everyone in Melbourne brought their own bags back to the grocery store. Australians already knew what I had yet to learn, that our everyday choices, like throwing away a plastic bag, added up to big consequences for our environment.

We went to Melbourne because my husband had a project there, a movie he was producing entitled *Ghostrider*. While he had exciting work to look forward to, my daughters and I only knew what we were leaving behind. Admittedly, we were reluctant travelers.

I was leaving my job as an English teacher at Harvard-Westlake School, an elite high school in Los Angeles. I loved my job and had fought for it. I grew up in Salt Lake City, white and well off, in a genteel middle-American world where I was never expected to do anything. When, after getting married, I worked my way through graduate school and took a job teaching high-school English, I was defying expectations. I became the first working mother in my family. It was a point of pride for me, so leaving it didn't come easy.

The November before, when I asked the head of my English Department for family leave, he replied: If there is a job when you come back, you can apply. I figured I was fired, but I knew family was first, so reluctantly, I gave notice.

For me, the thought of days on end with nothing on my schedule except dinner was scary to say the least. I decided to approach it the same way I approached my job. If I was going to be a stay-at-home mom, I was going to be the best stay-at-home mom I could be.

It was a philosophy that I took from a story that Nora Ephron once told me. Apparently, when Nora's mother was in the hospital giving birth to a younger sister, Nora's grandmother took her out to lunch. Nora wasn't sure about having a little sister. She liked things the way they were. Her grandmother said: Well, if you're going to be a big sister, you might as well be the best big sister ever. Nora took this advice to heart. When she told me this story, Nora claimed that it became a guiding principle for her life. As soon as I heard it, I adopted it too.

As I set off for Australia, I wasn't really sure what moms did all day at home, but I was determined to find out. There would be a hot breakfast before school. I would show up for parent–teacher association (PTA) events. I was going to fit in, make friends, and if nothing else, I vowed to read all the Homeric epics and *Anna Karenina*.

Standing at the grocery store on that first day, I had to figure out what to say to the cashier who asked me that baffling question: Would you like a bag? I was jetlagged and grumpy, and my first impulse was to be sharp with her. Of course I wanted a bag! Luckily, before I responded, I remembered my intention to be the best stay-at-home mom in Australia. I looked around for a clue about what I was expected to say.

The woman in front of me had her groceries packed in neat, square, green bags that looked vaguely like canvas but lighter. The woman behind me had an armful of the same bags. Obviously, the cashier expected me to say, No thanks, I have my own. But I didn't. Then I noticed a stack of those very same green bags on a hook right at the front of the conveyor belt for 99 cents. I put two of them on the belt and said, I'll just take these. I had no idea why everyone seemed to have their own bags; I just knew they did. Expectations are powerful, and I wanted to fit in. If that meant bagging my groceries

*Expectations are powerful.*

in green bags, so be it.

Back at our new place, I noticed that the only trash can in the kitchen was a minuscule round bin under the kitchen sink, about the size of my bathroom trash bin at home. I figured I'd have to take it out a few times a day, but oh well. I guessed that's just what Australian moms did. Not sure what to do with the green bags once they were empty, I left them by the front door and went to take a much needed nap. Oddly, I didn't have to take the trash out after filling up the fridge, which normally I did after a trip to the store in Los Angeles. But I was tired and didn't notice much.

Gary left for work the next morning and the girls went to school. There was a welcome lunch for parents, where I met a few other moms who would become my friends. Later that day, as she came home from school, Daryn noticed the green bags by the front door.

Can I have one of these for my school stuff? she asked as she breezed in.

Sure, I said.

Not to be outdone, Kayla said, Me too!

Okay, I said. I figured they were 99 cents in Australian currency, which at the time was about 75 cents US, so it was an easy give. My first bags disappeared, and I bought two more the next day.

On day three, Gary noticed the green bags lying by the front door as he was leaving for the set. Can I have one of these for my scripts?

Gary is always reading scripts, and this was before they were PDFs on iPads. They were 120 pages each on average, so a few of them were like carrying around a ream of paper. Sure, I said.

Before long, I owned six or eight of these green bags and we were using them to haul around all kinds of things.

What is it with these green bags? I asked my new friend Kim as we met not long after for a walking date.

Kim answered: The government is doing a whole push on reusable bags. I guess the old plastic ones are bad for the environment. They sent everyone fridge magnets and everything.

To me, that seemed like a plausible explanation, even though I hadn't seen any fridge magnets where we were staying. I remembered back in the 1980s when plastic bags with handles suddenly became ubiquitous. That was my year of living in New York City, and I recalled seeing articles about how bad plastic bags would be for the environment but also, how much better they were than paper bags. They didn't break even when wet, at least not if they weren't overloaded. That was a big consideration if you were walking on the street with groceries in bad weather, as millions of New Yorkers did almost daily. Stores began packing no more than two or three items per bag to avoid breakage. The voices objecting to the environmental impacts faded away, and plastic bags became the norm.

Because I considered myself an environmentalist, I never quite accepted plastic bags. I used them occasionally, but when I was asked paper or plastic, it was always paper for me. Living in Los Angeles and using a car for grocery shopping, paper was an easy choice. Paper bags were biodegradable, and you could recycle them. I was big on recycling. Even before curbside recycling pickup in Los Angeles, I collected bottles, cans, and newspapers in big bins, and once a week, packed them into the car with my kids for our trip to the recycling center. My kids had fun sorting different-colored glass bottles into the different bins. When curbside recycling came, I was relieved, but it wasn't as much fun.

In Australia, everyone seemed to be an environmentalist. They were several years into a historic drought at the time, so water restrictions were in place. You would be fined if your sprinklers hit the sidewalk or a stone walkway. As I was to learn, the sun really was more intense in Australia because the hole in the ozone was right above it. Most people over a certain age had large purple scars or splotches on their face, scalp, neck, and often on their hands and arms too, where cancerous lesions had been taken off. I'd heard some early predictions about global warming and how our climate was predicted to change. It seemed a long way off, hundreds or maybe thousands of years. In Australia, global warming was not a theoretical construct. They were already feeling the impacts.

We're the canary in the coal mine, my friend Penny told me over lunch not long after. She is an adamant environmentalist, almost alarmed even then.

I had a lot of time on my hands, so I spent some of it looking up the government's campaign for reusable bags. There were some statistics and nice fridge-magnet graphics, but the impetus seemed to come from a report the government had done on plastic bags.[14] It was a huge report, over 300 pages, and I found it compelling. I read the whole thing, line for line, word for word, the way I was reading *Anna Karenina* and, a month later, the Homeric epics. Having earned a Ph.D. in English, I was trained to read, study, and retain information, so I couldn't help it. I took the report to heart and committed it to memory, along with Anna, Dido, Odysseus, and the rest.

The 300-page report commissioned by the Australian government on the impacts of plastic bags was an important, groundbreaking study of the way that plastic reaches into every corner of our lives. Its findings have been widely corroborated by governments around the world. As I sat there reading it, I was, by turns, angry, shocked, dismayed, saddened, and flabbergasted that plastic was affecting everything around me in ways that were largely hidden from view. The hiding of these facts seemed to me purposeful and intentional, possibly nefarious.

As with everything else I had ever read, I was emotionally involved. Even though it was mostly a bunch of scientific analyses and big tables of data, all filled with technical terms that I didn't always understand, in my mind the tragic life of a plastic bag began to take shape. No wonder everyone in Australia had taken up the cause, and in Ireland too. My only wonder was, why hadn't America done the same?

Because I was a paper bag user, I was pretty smug reading about the effects of plastic bags on the environment. I was not so smug reading about the impacts of paper bags. The process of making them emitted four times more global-warming emissions than plastic bags, and transportation was also far more polluting than that for plastic bags. Also, I was shocked to learn that they didn't biodegrade in landfills, where about 80% of them ended up. To biodegrade, oxygen is required, but as items in a landfill become buried under more trash, the upper layers shut out air. Some studies of landfill suggested that newspapers from the 1920s were still readable if you were to dig down deep enough to find one. Presumably, paper bags from decades before remained there too.

I was furious. Here I thought I'd been making a choice that was better for the environment, and all the while I was contributing more emissions than if I used plastic! In my mind, I saw all the paper bags I had taken over the years, stacks of them. I felt duped. It really got me steamed.

I slammed drawers around the house for about a week. My kids and Gary became a little wary of me and listened to my harangues about how the whole recycling thing is just an excuse for overconsumption. The more I read and studied the report, the angrier I got. And I had a lot of time to read. I decided that

Australia had gotten it right. Paper or plastic? was the wrong question. Ireland had already taxed plastic bags out of use in 2002, three years earlier, and now Australia was all about getting rid of bags without a tax, and it was working. When I thought about the US and the waste we were generating, I was ashamed. Why wasn't anyone talking about this in the US?

I made great friends in Australia as did my kids and Gary. When it came time to leave in June, we were sick about it. The people were so open-hearted and eager to make friends. There were so many good restaurants, quirky shops, and dazzling local artwork. We'd taken weekend outings and watched with amazement as kangaroos and wallabies grazed on the lawn at dusk and dawn. We saw koalas feeding on eucalyptus trees by the Great Ocean Road and gazed at the Twelve Apostles, a group of limestone stacks off the coast of southern Australia rising 150 feet over the waterline, left over by erosion from some ice age eons ago. As we packed up to leave, we wanted to take so many things with us besides memories.

Secretly, though, the one thing I knew I couldn't live without was what I started calling, those damn bags. The last couple of weeks that I was there, I picked up a few from several different stores. Some were shorter and squatter, some taller and thinner. Some had more-than-one-color logos emblazoned on them, and some were not green but maroon or other colors. I happened into a wonderful kitchen store called The Essential Ingredient, an Aussie version of Williams Sonoma. There I found lovely navy-blue bags. They were of the taller, thinner shape, and the fabric seemed smoother, stronger, thicker. They were $1.99, but I had to have them, so I grabbed a few. I figured there was a good chance that I might not get my job back, and besides talking about books, I was suddenly passionate about reusable bags. Maybe there was something I could do with this in the States. I didn't know what, but I filled about half a suitcase with them. Gary looked at me like I was nuts, but he didn't say anything.

Just before we left Australia, I had lunch with Kim. I told her I was thinking about trying to promote reusable bags in the US, but I had no idea how to go about it. She laughed and told me about her brother, Peter Alexander, who was, as she called him, the pajama king of Australia.

According to Kim, after school, her brother Peter had a hard time finding a job. A really hard time. McDonald's had turned him down. He was demoralized, but his mother was encouraging and told him over and over that she believed in him.

One day, he walked into a clothing shop and asked about working there. The manager thought, *A gay guy, that might work.* So she hired him. He was a good salesman, and within a few months he asked if he could design a manikin display. Sure, she said. He did, and the outfit sold out immediately. So he did another one. Whatever he put on the manikin, it sold out in days, and soon she had him doing the shop windows.

It wasn't long before the manager got a call from the corporate office. What's going on there? Your sales are through the roof!

To her credit, the manager said, It's this guy I hired. He's doing our displays and they are genius.

Peter was brought into corporate and started designing windows company wide, and then he moved into product design and sourcing.

One night, he was talking to his mother (he was still living at home), who was not happy about her pajamas. Apparently, Aussie pajamas were all for old women, and she knew she was an old woman, but she didn't want to look like one. Why couldn't anyone make pajamas that felt more modern?

Peter immediately imagined modern pajama sets for women. He went to his company and told them he wanted to develop the idea. They let him design and start sourcing them. He had some on order when, for some reason I don't remember, the company decided that modern pajamas wouldn't work, and they canceled the order. Peter was incredulous. Instead of accepting the decision, he quit and acquired the order directly from the vendor.

This was in early fall, and Kim said she remembered when they took the order into her mom's house. There were boxes everywhere. They made corridors between the boxes to get from the living room to the kitchen to the bedrooms. But Peter's mother and Kim both kept telling him to keep going, so he got some photographs taken with models and put ads in the local newspaper in Melbourne. Good-looking pajamas for women just before Christmas.

As soon as the ad appeared, their mother's phone started ringing. Everyone pitched in, even his mom, taking orders on yellow pads, boxing and shipping pajamas in the evenings. He sold out before Christmas. Peter ordered more PJs for spring, moved out of his mother's house, and became a premier pajama brand in Australia and still is. It was a great story, super-inspiring. Miracles can happen.

**Chapter 3**

# Use What You Know

The Australian report on plastic bags gave me a focus for a feeling I already had about sustainability and our way of life. I don't remember what I was reading or hearing about global warming in those days, but whatever it was, it felt true to me.

I know it sounds wishy-washy to say that the information *felt true*. We are supposed to be able to distinguish between facts and beliefs. Facts are true whether we believe them or not. Beliefs are ideas we have about the world which may or may not be based in fact. However, it's easy to confuse one with the other. Although we like to think of ourselves as rational and reasonable, the real truth is that how we feel about something is often much more important than what we know about it.

> *How we feel about something is often much more important than what we know about it.*

In any case, the Australian report on retail bags fit the facts as I knew them and awakened in me a feeling commensurate to those facts. It made me want to help other people feel the way I did about plastic bags.

My curiosity drove me to further research, and I discovered very different stories about how Australia and Ireland had gone reusable. In Ireland, rapid economic growth in the 1980s and 1990s was accompanied by a rising litter rate. Over 60% of tourists reported that the streets of Ireland were dirtier than at home.[15] Ireland's Minister for the Environment said as early as 1999: The day of the plastic bag is coming towards an end.[16]

Ireland commissioned a group of scientists to come up with the best alternative. The result of their work: the 99 cent reusable bag made from non-woven polypropylene (NWPP) that everyone is now familiar with all over the world. It uses the resources of 11 plastic bags, holds the equivalent of 4 to 5 plastic-film bags, and is designed for a hundred or more uses. Also, it's machine washable, cold water, line dry. Used twice a week for a year, a couple of reusable bags can replace a thousand single-use plastic bags. Even when you add in ocean shipping, the potential for reducing emissions and waste is enormous.

Ireland imposed a 15-cent levy on plastic bags in early 2002, calling it a plas-tax. It was a spectacular success. Three months later, plastic bag use dropped 90%, and the government had raised 3.5 million euros in tax revenue dedicated to cleaning up the environment.[17]

Australia's path to plastic bag reduction was quite different. Noting the success of the Irish plas-tax, ministers in Australia set out to fund their own study. Delving deeper than the visible effects of plastic litter, the government report examined what plastic was made of, how it was made and where, transportation costs, emissions, and did a thorough comparison of the entire life cycle of over a dozen types of bags from creation to usage to disposal. Some were too unwieldy. Some were too expensive for mass adoption. Some, like the cotton bag, were associated with high levels of pollutants like pesticides and bleach.

The report was exhaustive in its research, and the results were clear. Reusable bags were better in every metric and Ireland had developed the most practical reusable bag at the most reasonable cost with the least damage to the planet.

Armed with this information, Australia did not propose a tax. They brought leaders from retail stores together with local government officials to hash out a plan. To avoid a tax, grocery stores and other retailers agreed to three measures:

- Offer reusable NWPP bags and display them prominently at checkout for no more than 99 cents.

- Refuse a free bag for people purchasing three items or fewer.
- Change the question at checkout from paper or plastic to: Would you like a bag?

That key question, the one the cashier asked me on my first day in Australia, was really part of a large government initiative that had started with science and ended in strategy. They leveraged what they knew to be powerful beyond taxes—social capital, in other words, expectations.

The government mounted a massive campaign dedicated to promoting reusable bags. This was an action that every Australian could take to get things moving in the right direction. It was cheap. It was easy. Yes, fridge magnets were mailed out. Most people admitted, the reusable bags were better. They broke less and held more. They didn't hurt your hands even with heavy items. Because you could sling a bag or two over your shoulder, they were easier to carry. No more trips back and forth from the car to the kitchen. And no bags to dispose of when you're done. Suddenly, you could fill up your fridge without filling up your garbage can or some side cabinet with plastic bags. It was an easy switch to go reusable, and most Australians did.

When we returned to the US, I was thankful that Harvard-Westlake offered me my job back. It was June, so I had a whole summer in front of me before buckling down to work. Being a teacher gave me roughly the same vacations as my kids. Many families have a place they like to vacation that becomes more familiar over time. For us, that place is Martha's Vineyard, where we'd been spending a few weeks every summer since the mid-1990s. After a handful of seasons, I had a large and well-developed group of friends with whom I was very close.

When the summer season on Martha's Vineyard begins, we all ask each other the same question: How was your winter? In

2005, my answer was all about Australia—the people, koalas, wallabies, and kangaroos, but mostly, reusable grocery bags. How everyone in Australia was using them, how I started using them, the whole life of a plastic bag, how it touched everything we knew, including the ocean and our health. We would look out over the ocean with a new appreciation of the growing problems there. I told them that we had to go reusable here in the US. It's crazy not to, I said. And my friends agreed.

I'd brought some reusable NWPP bags back with me, but not nearly enough for every friend who wanted one. Searching the internet, I couldn't find a single NWPP bag in the whole US. There was a phone number for a company called Green Bag with a parent company in Ireland. I called them repeatedly, and finally someone called me back saying they had no staff. It was an exploratory office. I suspected it was just a phone number.

I had a fantastic book group on Martha's Vineyard then. There were about a dozen women in the group, mostly from Boston, but also from Ojai, New York City, Albuquerque, Washington DC, and elsewhere. For years, it was the highlight of our week, a day to convene with other women, explore new thoughts, be taken seriously for our opinions, and talk about stories.

My book-group friends were the first to hear about what I'd learned about plastic bags. At the beach or at dinner parties, there was little else I wanted to talk about.

We have to go reusable, I repeated to anyone who would listen.

One day, a friend turned to me and said: No, Lisa, we don't have to do anything. *You* have to do it. You are obsessed! Right then, I had the feeling that this was a challenge I was meant to take on.

Another friend in my book group had started a nonprofit the year before. I remember sitting with her at the beach as she was writing in a notebook. When I asked, What are you working on? she said, A business plan. To me, it sounded fantastically romantic to be sitting on a beach writing a business plan. It was ambitious. Then I thought to myself, *I can write. I'll see if I can write a business plan.* I started thinking about what I would want to create if I did create something. The mission was clear: to convince Americans to switch to reusable bags. At first, I thought I would start up a nonprofit. That idea didn't get very far with me. First of all, how could they go reusable if the best reusable bag alternative wasn't available? Besides, I would have to raise money, and if there's one thing I'm not comfortable doing, it's asking people for money.

Then it occurred to me that I could sell bags to fund a campaign to get people to go reusable. That seemed like a better pathway. Ideally, I thought, I would make the bags in America. Again, this idea didn't get very far. I had no idea what the fabric was made of, how it was made, how a sewing factory works, or how to print on it. Assuming I could learn or hire people who could do those jobs, there would be a significant investment in machinery and factory space. The kind of money I didn't have. Who would give an English teacher enough money to invest in a manufacturing facility to make a product that had no proven market in the US? If that's what I wanted, I would have to give up the whole thing.

In the end, I felt that sourcing from overseas was not a moral compromise as long as I ensured fair working conditions wherever I found a manufacturer. I vowed to treat everyone in my supply chain fairly and I kept that promise to the end. If I succeeded, I hoped homegrown manufacturers would emerge, and later they did, creating jobs in the US. I dedicated myself to educating American consumers about the impacts of disposable bags and offering them a better bag.

As a concept, importing and selling bags to fund my campaign to convince Americans to switch to reusable bags sounded promising. I was fully aware even then that there was much I didn't know. I'd never run a business. I had no idea how to source an item or import it. I didn't know anything about shipping, bookkeeping, marketing, and all the other things I would learn piece by piece over the next few years. At that moment, there seemed to be a yawning cliff of stuff I didn't know. I needed advice.

I went to my friend Laurie David. I had known Laurie for a number of years on the Vineyard. Laurie and I were both passionate about the environment and were avid readers. Laurie would become a huge influence and supporter of mine. She has a deeply rooted sense of ethics and an ability to envision a better world. She also has a passion for acting on her beliefs. She not only offered me encouragement then, but she later promoted me in powerful ways as my business got started.

Laurie was the genius behind the campaign to put Hollywood stars in Prius cars to arrive at the Oscars as PR for hybrid vehicles. She was incredibly connected, and by 2005 she had turned most of her attention to the environment. We went for a walk, and I talked about my time in Australia, how far ahead they were in so many environmental areas. She listened as we wound our way down the trail to the beach. It was morning, our kids were at camp. Sun filtered through the trees as we switched back left and right down the ravine. I talked about the historic drought, the hole in the ozone, the cancerous splotches on the elderly, and bags—the impacts, the 99 cent reusable bags, the oceans filling up with plastic.

Maybe, I said, I should start a campaign to get people to pay attention to the little things we do every day that add up to big impacts on the environment.

She was thoughtful, but eventually she said, You don't have to do everything. In fact, you can't. Finally at the shore, we looked out on the sun shining on the water, and she said the words that would motivate me for the next few years. Just do one thing. That bag thing. You should do it.

But there are so many things to do, and I've never done

anything like this, I replied.

Look, she said, you're asking my opinion, and I'm telling you. Just do one thing. That bag thing — do it.

It was like what my other friend had said to me: *You* have
to do it. At another time, I might have

*Just do one thing.* said, No, I'm going back to teaching.

But now, thinking I'd been fired gave me a chance to see myself as something other than an English teacher. At the time, I didn't know what, but the idea began to take shape. That bag thing. I should do it. So, I set out to see what it would take.

I spent a few days in deep thought, trying to figure out how I could go about such a thing as changing American shopping culture. The US was not Australia or Ireland. Our economy wasn't driven by tourism. Global warming was a tenuous theory, not a reality, not even widely accepted. I wanted Americans to choose reusable bags, but I needed to give them a reason.

As I would do many times in starting up my business, I used what I knew, and what I knew best was literature and literary theory. When I was getting my Ph.D. in English, I learned that old stories, like mythology and folklore, revealed deep belief systems and social codes, in other words, expectations. For example, I knew that the many stories about a series of impossible tests to win the hand of a princess came down from the days of warrior cultures. When royal sons were expected to be warriors, too many were lost to make them a viable vehicle for lineage. So, royal blood was passed down through daughters who remained safe behind castle walls. Men able to manage a castle and all that came with it were wanted to marry princesses. Tests of cleverness, loyalty, and strength were required.

Mythical beasts and impossible creatures were symbols of cultural change. As people migrated, they brought their beliefs with them and grafted new beliefs onto local beliefs in order to gain acceptance. For example, tens of thousands of years ago, the people who first developed language and stories were hunter-gatherers who believed in various animal cults. Bird cults, bear cults, wolf cults, and the like. Later, as people domesticated horses, horse cults sprang up. We don't really know what happened when the people of the horse cults rode up and met the people of the bird cults. Did they fight? Probably. What we do know is that at some point, we come across images of a horse with wings: Pegasus.

When cultures clash, images of impossible beasts and fantastical creatures emerge. A dragon, a sphinx, a minotaur. Successful cultures did not entirely destroy the beliefs of their enemies. It was more effective to co-opt those beliefs, graft them onto your own, and by giving your enemy something familiar to hang on to—a wing, a lion's foot, a bull's horn—tell a story to win them over. Impossible heroes and fantastical beasts helped knit two cultures together in imagination as a result of two cultures coming together in fact. To ancient people, they weren't myths at all. They were real stories of cultural change.

It probably didn't hurt that I had been reading the Homeric epics. Odysseus with Circe and the men who turned into pigs. Demi-gods and goddesses. Stories are how we explain cultural change. As I thought about all this, I thought, *Maybe, just maybe, I could spin a tale of a new mythical being: a reusable grocery bag.*

As I sat at my kitchen table in Martha's Vineyard, I began to stitch together the tragic story of a plastic bag from the facts in the Australian report. I knew that the role of tragedy is to sweep away the old to make place for the new. So, I spun a tale where the plastic bag was the tragic hero, doomed to die. The new mythical hero would be the reusable bag. A bag that didn't break, didn't hurt your hands, didn't fill up your garbage bin, didn't destroy our oceans. A bag that created zero waste for up to a year and could be recycled at the end of a long and useful life. In short, a mythical bag of heroic proportions. Americans don't particularly like facts and figures and are generally opposed to taxes. And yet, having a filmmaker for a husband, I knew that Americans love a good story.

I developed the story of the tragic life of a plastic bag pretty much as I laid it out at the beginning of this book, though for my purposes here, I have updated some of the facts and figures. In 2005, I wasn't able to say that the plastic we were throwing away was coming back to us on our plates and what it was doing to our bodies. It would be another ten years before we knew that a quarter of all fish sold in markets had ingested plastic.[18] By 2017, two thirds of the fish in our food supply were estimated to be contaminated by plastic ingestion.[19] About the same time, studies began to show evidence of endocrine disruption in large fish and mammals in the wild. Just recently, scientists have begun to document the toxic effects of plastic exposure in humans, including gender abnormalities and precipitous drops in sperm counts.[20] Back then, I saw that all those effects would be a possibility, but I ended the story a little earlier than I do now. Still, it's essentially the same story.

So, there I was, with a tragic story and a mythical hero. The question was, would anyone care if I told them the tragic story of a plastic bag? Would anyone imagine a new future with a mythical reusable bag? I wasn't sure I was convinced, but it was the best tool I had at the time. By mid-summer, I was willing to try.

## Chapter 4

# Write a Business Plan

Over the summer of 2005, I perfected my story. I started telling everyone I met what happens to plastic bags and how reusable bags could save literally billions of bags from the same fate. Honestly, I was surprised that I met with such interest. Nearly everyone said they would buy a bag from me if I had one to offer them. The message was, Go for it! Even Rosabeth Moss Kanter, a professor at Harvard Business School who is a longtime friend and member of my book club, said, Go, Lisa!

It's one thing to have a mission, a story, and a lot of passion. It's another thing to start a business. Luckily, when I mentioned to my friends that I had no idea what I was doing, many of them offered their networks to help.

One of my book-group friends offered the advice of her husband. He was a consultant and entrepreneur and she said he'd be happy to help. I invited him over for lunch as an incentive. Looking back, I should have just offered him a coffee. Lunch is too long if things don't go well, and things did not go well.

About ten minutes into lunch, as he sat there listening to me, he got a terrible look on his face. I don't remember exactly what he said—I think I blanked out—but he let me know in no uncertain terms that this idea would never work. Americans did not reuse bags and would not buy them. It was a terrible idea for a business and sure to fail. He couldn't leave fast enough.

In the years to come, to his credit, he and I had a good laugh about how well things turned out for me. More than once as I would run into him at a dinner party, I detected a look on his face that I would come to recognize, somewhere between admiration and disbelief, but mostly disbelief.

Anyway, after he rushed out of my house that day, I sat

down to figure out what had just happened. My women friends loved the idea, were all willing to pay for a bag, and many had already started to limit the number of bags they were taking at the store. Was this a guy thing? Was it a business thing? I wasn't sure how I would find out, but I determined to keep going.

I went for a walk soon after with another friend from my book group, one of my closest friends and biggest supporters. She said, Why don't you go see my cousin, Michael? Michael and his wife Andrea have a home on Martha's Vineyard not far from mine. He too is a business consultant and couldn't have been nicer. Michael and Andrea invited me to coffee at their place and we all sat comfortably on couches with a warm cup. My visit with them was pretty much the opposite of my visit a few days earlier, and it turned out to be the key to unlocking the first doors to starting a business. Michael and Andrea worked to put me at ease as I sat there explaining how I'd found these bags in Australia, how everyone there and in Ireland was using them, and launched into an early version of my tale of a plastic bag. Although I was not as polished as I would be later, the story I told made an impact on them as we sat looking out their windows at the nearby ocean shimmering in the morning light.

Michael asked good questions about why people would pay for a product that they could get for free. I talked about what I had learned in the report. I mentioned that Seventh Generation labels calculated how many thousands of pounds of toxic chemicals would be reduced if every household in America replaced their petrochemical dishwashing liquid with their plant-based version. I told Michael that I wanted to focus on the impact one person made, not the impact of all bags in the US put together. Those numbers were too big, too overwhelming.

For example, I explained to him, the Australian report had a chart that explained the amount of energy that it took to manufacture a single disposable plastic bag. The energy was measured in megajoules or MJ. That was a new term for me, but the report explained. A megajoule is the amount of energy it takes to heat 3 liters of water to boiling point. Three liters is enough to make 12 cups of coffee or tea. According to the report, it takes 0.48 MJ to produce a single plastic grocery bag, including materials and manufacturing. It was pretty simple math. Just under a half a megajoule meant that the energy it took to make one bag was enough to heat about six cups of coffee or tea.

Of course, cups of tea are not likely to help people make a connection between a bag and global warming. Investigating further, I discovered that an average car consumes 4.18 MJ driving 1 kilometer. It dawned on me that I could measure the amount of energy in bags as a driving equivalent. If it takes 4.18 MJ to drive 1 kilometer, that was just under the equivalent of the energy used by nine bags. Converting this to miles, I calculated that 14 plastic bags use the same energy as it takes to drive a car 1 mile, and in both cases, that energy was derived from petroleum. That was a statistic I could work with.

Michael was one of the first people to ask me details about the impacts of bags, and I gave him the petroleum equivalent of bags to miles driven. I said I wanted people to know their actions mattered. At the time, studies showed that consumers used an average of ten plastic bags a week per person. Two people living together brought home enough plastic bags every week to drive their car over a mile. Every week! I told him: I want people to think about the impacts of one bag at a time and make a decision based on what that bag means to them.

When I was done, Michael took a minute to think. Then he said, I don't know if this will work in America or not. But if it could work, you need a tipping-point strategy.

I had to ask: Tipping point? What's that?

It's a book by Malcolm Gladwell. If your idea is going to work, it needs to follow *The Tipping Point*. Andrea nodded encouragingly.

Michael suggested that I read the book first and then come back to him if I wanted to take it to the next step.

Within minutes of getting home, I bought the book on Amazon. I also bought 1bagatatime.com and onebagatatime. com. I wasn't sure I would use any of it, but these were small investments. Both paid off more than I could have imagined at the time.

Reading *The Tipping Point*, I realized that it gave me a marketing plan. Gladwell proposed a theory for starting a trend that entailed three essential factors:

- Stickiness
- Super-connectors
- Context

Although I wasn't sure that reusable bags were a sticky idea, it certainly had stuck with me. It was sticking pretty well with my friends too. Apparently, it had been sticky in Ireland, Australia, South Africa, and Bangladesh—everywhere that this reusable bag was introduced. I thought, *It just might be sticky enough in the US*. It wasn't out of the question.

The next thing I needed was a super-connector. I had a great group of friends, but trying to reach consumers across America? I needed more than a friendship group. Or so I thought at the time. Later I would discover that the people and places in my life gave me plenty of access to people whose reach was far greater than I could have dreamed of that summer of 2005. Over the next decade, I never turned down an opportunity to connect with new people and tell them about reusable bags, and I found a surprising number of willing listeners in places farther away than I would have guessed. All that networking would come later.

Then I emailed Michael and told him I would work on a tipping-point strategy. I thought that the context was maybe a little early, but if Priuses were going to the Oscars, reusable bags might not be far behind. I was willing to try.

Then Michael did a remarkable thing. He sent me an email walking me through the first few steps of starting my business. I say it was remarkable because Michael is a very good business consultant, and his advice was a gift. A generous one at that, and I've never forgotten it. It might have taken him a few minutes or maybe half an hour, but I'm forever grateful to Michael and so many other friends, as I will tell later, for the success I was able to achieve. Without them, I would have stumbled and lost the moment.

Besides creating a tipping-point campaign, Michael told me to build a library of facts and figures. I had a definitive 300-page report, so that was easy. The next item he mentioned made me pause. He told me to acquire expertise and inventory in reusable bags.

I took Michael's advice seriously. I felt that if someone was going to be generous with good advice, the least I could do was take it. So, I sat down to figure out how to acquire expertise and inventory. I'd already worked hard

*If someone was going to be generous with good advice, the least I could do was take it.*

to find someone selling bags in the US and came up with nothing. I needed to import them. Probably from China.

A lot of what I did up until that point had some reference or relevance to my history or education. But importing from China? That was another wheelhouse altogether.

Poking around on Google, I soon found Alibaba.com. It looked like Amazon.com but for wholesale commodity goods. There were dozens of sellers of green bags there. At first I thought, *Maybe this won't be so hard after all. Maybe I can acquire bags from China the way I ordered books from Amazon.* Unfortunately, international sourcing turned out to be a lot harder. I read the pitch for seller after seller. Many of them had an English version that was somewhat readable. There seemed to be minimum order quantities for everything, including bags. Minimum orders on some sites were 10,000, on others 25,000, still others 50,000. What would I do with 10,000 bags? The numbers seemed impossible.

But I had already gone this far into the realm of impossible things, so I just kept going. I contacted a few sellers as if I were serious. I wasn't sure I was, but it didn't cost me much to pretend. On the website form for a few companies selling bags, I typed in that I was starting a company to sell reusable bags in the US and could they answer the following three questions:

- What is the price?
- What is the minimum order quantity?
- Can you arrange shipping to the US?

They needed to arrange shipping from China to the US because I wasn't ready to acquire expertise in international shipping. That would come later. I was getting a little overwhelmed as it was.

A few days later, there was no answer. I went back to Alibaba and reached out to more sellers, about a dozen this time, and the next day a few dozen. Still no reply. I was mystified. Why wouldn't they respond to a buyer? Later I would learn about Chinese manufacturers and how they thought. The Chinese were selling these bags by the million to Australia, Ireland, and elsewhere, but not the US. A minimum order of bags to the US probably just looked weird to them. I would come to see this as typically Confucian. Hear no evil, see no evil. If it seems weird, look the other way and maybe it will just go away. I would see my Chinese friends do this in the many years I visited China, just look the other way when anything wasn't going according to plan. Usually, the problem did just go away. It wasn't my style, but I had to hand it to them—often it worked and avoided a lot of confrontation.

But back at my computer, I was stumped. How could I

acquire inventory if I couldn't get a seller to reply to me? As I pondered the problem, I looked at my bags from Australia. For the first time, I started looking closely. Eventually, I came to The Essential Ingredient bag, the upscale bag that cost me $1.99. The fabric seemed heftier. Some of the other bags flopped over when you opened them, but this one stood up straight, easier for loading. I looked inside and, to my surprise, near the bottom, I noticed a little white tag sewn into a seam with a website printed on it.

Putting the website into Google, I was disappointed to find that it looked exactly like the other Chinese sites I had discovered on Alibaba. *Still*, I thought, *I'll try again*. I typed:

Hello, I found a bag of yours at The Essential Ingredient in Australia. I want to start a company to sell reusable bags like this in the United States. I would like to know: 1. What is the price? 2. What is the minimum order quantity? 3. Can you arrange shipping to the US? Thank you.

To my shock and surprise, there was an answer the following morning with a price, a minimum order quantity of 8000 bags, and assurance they could ship to the US. It was signed Amy. Beneath her name was a long address in a city called Changzhou. Immediately, I put the city into Google and found it on the map not too far from Shanghai.

That was the beginning of the friendship between me and Amy. She is to this day one of my best friends, someone I've come to know very well. When I try to explain my sense of kinship with Amy, I say that she is the Chinese me. Though everything about us—our lives, our circumstances, our histories, and our families—couldn't be more vastly different, we are very alike in ways that matter. Over the next 12 years, our fates and lives would become inextricably intertwined.

I replied to Amy right away. I had so many questions: What are the bags made of? NWPP, which is non-woven polypropylene. What size are they? 24 H x 27 W x 16 G cm. What does G stand for? Gusset, the side panel. What is that little piece of plastic on the bottom called and what does it do? It's called the bottom stiffener. It adds strength and helps the bag stand up. Can you make the handles longer? Sure. How much can you put in a bag like this? About 9 kg (19 lbs). How long will it last? Depends how you use it. Normally for groceries, it will last one to two years. How do you print on it? Screen printing.

And dozens of other questions. We went back and forth daily, me typing during my day, and she responding overnight when it was daytime for her. We began to get into a rhythm as I acquired expertise.

Amy had questions about me: Why do you want to start a bag business in America? It's the right thing to do for the environment. What business are you in? English teacher. Where will you sell them? I don't know, I'm still exploring.

I told her a little bit about my history, my husband being a movie producer, finding these bags in Australia, having a passionate desire to do something good for the environment. I asked about her. She started her career first as a model, then as an accountant, like her father. After that, she worked as an account representative for a bag exporter. Then one of her customers, John, helped her set up her own business as an exporter. In China, most factories don't have a license to export. Exporters work as a broker between factories that manufacture and sell goods and foreign buyers who want goods. John became her first client, sourcing bags for Australia where he was living.

Within a few weeks, I knew I would soon have to do something more than pretend. I would have to put real money down and place an order of bags. That brought up a whole new set of questions. How could I figure out if I could make money at it, or at least not lose any? How would I ship them to customers?

Customers?! How would I get customers?

I knew the selling price had to be 99 cents, but I needed to get real now about whether that would cover the costs of getting them and selling them. At a cocktail party, I was explaining my bag idea to my friend Bob Rosenberg. He was teaching at Babson College and had spent his career building Dunkin' Donuts into a powerhouse. I figured he would have good advice about how to write a business plan, and he did. He said to go to the Small Business Administration (SBA) website and find a resource there.

Bob was right. Browsing the SBA website, I found a tutorial for how to write a business plan. *Perfect*, I thought. It was a nice PDF with cute illustrations, using the example of Perky's Poodle Parlor. Write a mission statement, something like: to clean and clip the poodles of my neighborhood with utmost care and beautiful results. Something that would get you up in the morning and remind you what your business was about. Find a place of business, preferably not too close to your competition. Estimate your expenses: rent, bathing equipment and supplies, office equipment and an assistant or two, little perks to please customers like pink and blue bows, signage, and a front counter. Then develop your price list and calculate your profit. It was like a fifth-grade word problem: how many poodles do you need to clip to make, say, a thousand dollars? It was cute. It had nothing to do with international sourcing, but there was a structure there. It was a start.

The problem I was facing wasn't something you'd want to give a fifth grader: If the minimum order quantity is 8000, shipping and customs costs both internationally and domestically are unknown, and the maximum price per bag is 99 cents, how can I be sure I won't lose any money, or at least not much?

Following up with Michael, he again came through with a remarkable gift of advice that helped me translate poodle clipping into global supply terms. I still have his email. It went like this:

Dear Lisa

Whether or not you should order bags and can make money at it is not simply a projection. One way to get at an answer is to look at it from an ongoing business perspective.

An ongoing business would be based on the assumption that you have set up an organization that is capable of building and maintaining a reasonable volume of business, year after year. A very crude set of assumptions might be that you have hired the following people (annual cost estimate in brackets) to run such a business, giving you the Operating Costs:

- General Manager ($125K)
- Sales Manager ($75K)
- Operator (purchasing, logistics, $75K)
- Rent ($75K)
- Marketing, Travel, Events ($100K)
- Total Operating Cost Estimate $450K

Now you make assumptions on your Operating Margin, which is your revenue (number of bags sold x selling price) minus your product cost.

If you sell 1 million bags at $1 each, your revenue is $1m. If you pay $0.50 per bag, your product cost is $500k. Your Operating Margin then is $500k.

From your Operating Margin of $500k you would subtract your Total Operating Costs, which in this assumption is $450k.

Given these assumptions, the business would make a profit of $50k.

With this outline, you now can plug in different assumptions about costs and revenues and calculate the profitability of the business. It helps to think in terms of specific time periods, such as years.

That was helpful. I realized I had enough expertise already to turn some of my unknowns into realistic assumptions and financial projections. I opened a spreadsheet and put the presumed selling price of bags, 99 cents, and the quantity, 8000 bags, up at the top. Down below, I put in the cost of bags from Amy, multiplied that by the quantity, and then laid out other costs to create a formula that would calculate gross margin. I didn't have employees or rent at the time, so most of the costs had to do with shipping and customs. I weighed one bag and extrapolated what 100 bags would weigh. I added a bit for a box and put my assumptions into the FedEx site for an idea about what shipping would cost. The spreadsheet subtracted every expense from revenue, and I watched my bottom line.

It wasn't long before I ran into gaps of what I couldn't even presume to know. Amy had given me a price to the Port of LA. There was still the cost of customs and trucking to my house. And then, I had to ship them to customers. Michael suggested that I think in years, but at that time, I could only think in terms of a minimum order quantity, 8000 bags. Still, there were a lot of unknowns.

Later in my business, this spreadsheet would become an invaluable tool for me. It was a very real way for me to estimate the financial impact of a load of bags before I ordered them. Within a few years, I would learn how to extrapolate how many bags I was selling a month, and from there, calculate the cost per bag for my rent and my employees. As I became an experienced importer, it became more accurate. When more competition came into the field, I used it to get cutthroat competitive. Thanks to Michael and the SBA, I started to understand what a business model was.

At some point, I sat down to see if I could write a business plan. The mission statement was simple. Saving the world, 1 Bag at a Time. To be sure, it was audacious, perhaps grandiose. But I really saw it in those terms. It articulated why I would even try to do this work.

Then I decided to name the company 1 Bag at a Time. It was a little long, a little clunky, but there was a ring to it. No one was using that phrase back then. When I asked a friend in marketing if it was a good name, she told me to trademark it right away. I would work over the next decade to defend the trademark and try to get everyone else to stop using it. Clearly, other people thought there was a ring to it too.

Then, I needed a logo. Someone referred me to a graphic artist who created my first logo. I admit, it was a pretty bad logo. It looked like this:

Now, I see everything wrong with it. It's too vertical. It's, well, a little silly. But when he sent it over, I thought it was great. In any case, I didn't think about it too much. It said what I wanted it to say.

Now that I had a logo, I started to think about ordering bags. What color would they be? My friends in the book club all thought the green bags were hideous, and one friend, who owned a nice little clothing shop on the Upper West Side of Manhattan, suggested that I buy black bags.

Everyone likes a black bag, she said with assurance.

That was true, I thought. I started to think about an order of 8000 bags from China in black fabric with a white logo.

There was still a lot I didn't know, but I figured if I came close to breaking even on my first order, I would improve later. I started a spreadsheet to track my expenses. I listed the cost of registration for the website URL and the logo. Amy gave me a price per bag, including shipping to Los Angeles. I still needed someone to clear customs and drive them to me, but I was moving forward.

The closer I came, the more nervous I became. One night, falling asleep, I allowed myself to think what it would look like to be successful. I imagined supplying a bunch of grocery stores with reusable grocery bags. Instead of thinking about cleaner oceans, fewer emissions, happy clean households, I started to think about the business. Suddenly, I had a vision of boxes. What did a hundred thousand boxes look like? In my mind, it began to take shape. A warehouse. Forklifts. Men in hard hats. Those floodlights on the ceiling with little wire cages around them. Trucks and loading docks. It occurred to me that I had no place in a warehouse. I imagined myself, 5 feet 2 inches, standing there. It shook me awake and I started hyperventilating.

It woke up my husband. What's wrong? he asked.

Warehouses, I said. I'm thinking about warehouses.

He grunted and went back to sleep. I didn't fall asleep that night for a long time.

By now, it was early August. Classes started in September after Labor Day, but faculty meetings started two weeks earlier. Instinctively, I knew that if I didn't order bags before I went back to classes, there would be distractions and I probably would never do it. It was time to stop pretending and put down money.

Even though I didn't think I had any business in a warehouse, that bag thing still awoke in me a feeling that made my heart swell. It wasn't ambition, really. It was just something I had to do. A moral imperative coming from my small and fervent heart. If I tried hard enough, maybe I really could help save the world one bag at a time.

I knew everything that made it a long shot for me. Who was I to think that I could beat the odds? But deep inside, I believed that sooner or later, the US, like Australia and Ireland, would go reusable. Maybe, just maybe, I could be the one with the sticky idea. Why not me? If I was lucky, worked hard, and made good decisions, it was possible that I really could change the way America shopped. It was both exciting beyond words and terrifying in my bones.

I started plugging the numbers I knew into my spreadsheet. Besides the bags themselves, customs clearance, and trucking costs, I still had to pay for tags to be printed in Los Angeles. Some costs were still unthinkable, like shipping costs to customers, so I ignored them. I figured the whole load would cost me about $6000 to get them to my house. The number made me a little breathless. It was nearly double my monthly teacher's paycheck. For me, that was real money. Little did I know that within two years, I would be wiring sums to China larger than double my entire annual teacher's salary, which also made me hyperventilate, but that was later.

According to my spreadsheet, if my selling price was 99 cents, I'd make enough to have a thousand or so dollars for tags and shipping costs. This was possible. I wouldn't lose money, or at least not much. I could store them in my dining room since I didn't have a garage, and we hardly used the dining room anyway. I still had real problems, like how would I get customers? How would my husband react when I asked for $6000? What about my day job? Did I really have the courage to go through with this? I wasn't a quitter, but I had real doubts.

Those doubts swirled inside me as I went to my last book-club meeting of summer. Our last book club was always a little emotional, a signal that summer was ending. That week, I stuck to the book. No bag talk, no global warming, no 14 bags to drive a car a mile. We were reading poetry and I was fully focused.

It was my friend Mary who brought it up as we were saying goodbye. Mary had been an original member of my book club. Among her many accomplishments, she owned a chic boutique on Montana Avenue in Santa Monica. Always empathetic and tuned in, Mary saw the worry on my face and asked me about my bag project. I told her I wasn't sure I could do it. There was a minimum order quantity and it cost a lot of money. I was having doubts.

Well, how many is a minimum order? she asked.

Eight thousand bags, I said, as if the number were completely outrageous.

Without skipping a beat, she said, I'll take two thousand.

It was the least expected answer I could have imagined. I'm sure my face changed from doubt to sheer surprise. I had a customer! I said: Are you sure?

Absolutely, she said.

She never asked me what the price would be, or when I would deliver them. She just smiled and I knew, I couldn't let her down. I would place my first order within days.

*I knew I couldn't let her down.*

The next day I talked seriously to Gary, who asked good questions. No, I didn't have an importer yet. He suggested that I contact his friend's wife, who worked for a company that imported for Target. Indeed, a few weeks later, she introduced me to the freight forwarder I would work with for the next dozen years. Gary also asked me about profit, and I explained my calculations. Then I told him about Mary and my first sale.

I told him: I think I have to do it. I don't know if I'll ever make any money at this, but I promise not to lose any, or at least not much.

Then I said something that surprised even me: If I can get this started, my goal will be to replace my teaching salary within two years and double it within five.

My teaching salary, of course, was not impressive. Still, I don't know where I got the nerve to say I would double it. I could feel my fervent heart beating. If Peter Alexander could become the pajama king, maybe I could become the Bag Lady. His story lived inside me. I didn't say all that, but I could feel it. Gary saw it in my eyes.

Do it, he said. Gary always believed in me. That too was empowering. I knew that if I failed, he would catch me. And I knew he believed I wouldn't fail, and that too was inspiring. I wouldn't let him down either. For someone like me, used to low expectations, high expectations were like a drug. I would crave it and do anything to stoke that feeling.

That is how, by the end of summer vacation 2005, I placed my first order of bags from China and started wiring money to Amy. Now I had to return to LA, get back into the classroom, and figure out how to sell 8000 bags by November so I could host Thanksgiving dinner in my dining room.

## Chapter 5

# Learn to Dig In

My first order was a test of my survival skills and stick-to-itiveness. There was so much I needed to learn, while keeping up with the demands of my teaching schedule and family life. As an English teacher, I'd been a fan of learning things from books. What I needed to learn now would not be found in a book. Every day there were new challenges and I just had to stick my neck out and try.

For this, I reached back to my experiences in high school. I was fortunate to attend The Putney School, a boarding school in Vermont. Besides academics, the school has a working farm where students do chores. After lunch on my first day of orientation, an older student led a few of my new classmates and me to the barn. He marched me to a pigsty and handed me a pitchfork and bucket. The pig was out, but his leavings were clearly still there.

Welcome to Putney, said the student and walked away, taking the others to other pigsties.

I stood there for a moment putting two and two together. Here was a pile of pig shit. Here I was, holding a pitchfork and bucket.

The pigsty was clean 15 minutes later, but I was changed forever. I realized that no matter what I'm faced with, sometimes I just have to dig in. That lesson was useful to me now. I might not be the best pigsty cleaner—or box handler, tag designer, website designer, or whatever else came my way—but I trusted that if I dug in and did my best, I'd be good enough to get the job done.

As classes started in fall 2005, I was guided by my schedule. I taught high school English first, second, and third period. During my fourth-period break, I stepped out onto the stairs overlooking the faculty parking lot behind the English Department and sold grocery bags.

While I'd been prepping for classes, I was also prepping for my first sales calls. I knew that small natural food stores would be my best bet. The question was, how to get a list of them? I had to stop thinking like a consumer and start thinking like a vendor. A veteran of small, quirky natural food stores, I started googling my favorite natural food brands for a clue about how brands think. Somehow, I happened on the website for Brown Cow, an organic yogurt brand whose webpage conveniently listed stores where you could find their product. Looking at that list, I thought: *If you're selling organic yogurt, you're going to want reusable bags.*

I transcribed the list from the website to a tiny green spiral notebook that I found in a desk drawer, one store per page, just the way they were listed on the Brown Cow site, alphabetically by state. The book was small enough to fit in my palm and didn't attract notice from other teachers as I stepped away from my desk. From this list, I started cold calling and perfecting my story of the tragic life of a plastic bag, a very short version. It didn't take me long to learn that if I got to the right person at one of these small stores, they would listen to the impacts of bags on our environment for not more than a minute.

Then I would move right into the mythical hero part, saying something like: I have a product that can help solve this problem for 99 cents. It's a reusable bag made from a new technological fabric that has taken over ninety percent of the grocery bag market in every country where it's been introduced. It's washable and made to last up to a year. Imagine: a grocery bag that creates zero waste for up to a year. The response rate was far higher than most cold-calling lists yield. More than half my targets requested more information.

I started putting together a sales kit: a sales sheet with a few facts about bags, sales features, pricing, and a sample bag. I admit, the sales sheet was more like an English teacher handout than a professional sales sheet. There were too many words and not enough photos. At least I knew enough to have a promotion. In a small textbox with borders at the bottom, it said: Order by November First for Free Shipping. The truth was, I had no idea how much it would cost to ship a box of bags from my house to some store somewhere, so I didn't know how to price it. Also, while I had given up the idea of hosting Thanksgiving that year, I still wanted to sell them as quickly as possible. Visions of box tunnels between the rooms of my house haunted me at night.

Managers were asking for a sample bag, so I asked Amy to FedEx me a box of a hundred. She didn't charge for the bags, but I had to cover shipping. I established a FedEx account and recorded the expense on my spreadsheet. I asked for Essential Ingredient bags. They were navy with a white imprint on one side showing a graceful duck silhouette and the store name below it. For 99 cents, it was a pretty nice bag.

I learned how to answer questions from store managers by trial and error. One question that came up a lot was about pricing. If they were buying bags at 95 cents and selling them at 99 cents, how would they make a profit?

I answered that by asking: How much profit are you making on the grocery bags you have now?

That was enough to silence most of them. They knew they were losing money on bags, so breaking even was a fiscal win. After all, I was talking to the bag buyer, who knew the cost of bags maybe better than anyone else, and most of them felt compromised by purchasing plastic bags, even though for expense reasons they had to.

By making plastic bags seem free, bags themselves came to have no value at all to the consumer and were almost invisible to grocery shoppers. They were expected. People could overconsume, seemingly without noticing that their behavior benefited the plastic industry at the expense of our taxes and our environment. Customers at small natural food stores were already concerned about the global costs of emissions and pesticides and were gaining a growing awareness of the problems with plastic. Disposable diapers, for example, were highly controversial. Most of the managers I was talking to were willing to take a shot on a box of a hundred bags. For me, that was a testament to the stickiness of the idea. I would continue to work with prospective clients to make the argument about the importance of charging for bags in order to create value in the consumer's mind which would encourage them to bring the bag back. We needed to help consumers understand that this was good for the store, good for them, and good for the environment. I was thankful that my early customers were willing to try this at a break-even point. As my sales grew, my cost competitiveness would have to get sharper for me to stay in business, but for now, I was trying not to lose money, at least not much.

I started switching back and forth from English teacher to Bag Lady. Either way, I was steeped in tragedy. I taught *The Scarlet Letter* first period, *Macbeth* second period, then back to *The Scarlet Letter* for third period. Fourth period I would palm my little green notebook and step out onto the back staircase to make cold calls, telling buyers about the tragic life of a plastic bag. As it got cooler, I brought warmer jackets to work. Cold calls turned into follow-up calls. Follow-up calls turned into sales. I started a new spreadsheet to track sales.

Even among those early orders in 2005, some customers insisted on putting their logo on the bag. My first order of bags had my logo on one side only, leaving the other side for imprints if customers wanted it. Sometime in the fall, I googled screen printers and started calling around to find someone who could put an imprint on a polypropylene grocery bag. On the phone, all of them said yes, they could, and I vaguely remember a rainy late autumn day spent trudging to small screen printers all over the city, asking them to put something, any image at all, on the blank side of the bag. Nearly all of them came back with a more or less melted mess. But I kept going.

Eventually I came to a very dingy screen printer not far from Hollywood High School. I almost didn't go in, but a guy with a rainbow-striped beanie and a big smile emerged. I showed him some of the melted examples and he said, You need to cure this with very low, low heat. Wait.

About ten minutes later, he came back with a little imprint of a white heart on the bag. I told him I would be back in a few weeks when my merchandise arrived.

Sometime in mid-October, Amy reported that my order was ready to be shipped. I was relying on my new freight forwarder, Tony, to clear customs and get them trucked to me. Tony is a friendly guy, from China originally, with two American kids and a house in Palos Verdes. He has been importing his entire career and understands Chinese and American business practices very well. He taught me a lot about US customs and the bustling port located in Long Beach. I had a lot of questions. For one thing, the paperwork from Amy on the bag price said: FOB Los Angeles. I tried to look up FOB online and found a dizzying number of acronyms. Even when it was spelled out as Free on Board, I had no idea what it meant.

Tony was happy to explain. Free on Board names the place where the price applies. There is one price FOB Shanghai. Then you need to pay for shipping to Los Angeles. There is another price FOB Los Angeles. Shipping is included.

Now I understood.

Tony went on. This is a very important item, but many of my clients don't ask. I think you will be very good at this. You notice the right things.

I thanked him and hoped he was right. I was willing to take any encouragement I could get.

Eventually I got a call from Tony giving me a date for arrival.

I told him to deliver after 3 p.m. so I could get home from teaching. One Thursday in mid-November, a huge truck pulled up outside my house. The driver looked at me skeptically. Apparently, he wasn't used to dropping goods in nice, tree-lined neighborhoods. He had a lift-gate to lower the bags to the ground, but because of the slope of the road and driveway, he couldn't use it. I would have to pick the boxes off the back of the freight truck, one by one, and carry them to the house.

There were 400 boxes weighing about 40 pounds (18 kg) each. I suppose I should have been daunted, but this delivery was the culmination of months of planning, deliberating, and determination. I was so excited about finally getting my bags that I forgot to consider my own physical limitations. I lifted the first box and found that if I balanced it on my shoulder, I could get it up the driveway. I went back for the second. This was not going to be fast. My housekeeper was there that day, and she helped me carry a few, but she couldn't carry one alone, so she wasn't much help. I would bring the bags near the back door, and she started rolling them inside.

After about 15 minutes, my neighbor Michael came out. What are you doing? he asked.

I told him I was starting a reusable grocery bag business.

He looked at me blankly and then said, Well, let me help.

Together it took us about 45 minutes to get all the boxes up near the back door. Again, I found myself incredibly grateful for the generosity of a friend, and I bought Michael a bottle of wine as a thank-you. Throughout it all, the truck driver kept looking at me with an expression I was beginning to recognize, a mixture of admiration and disbelief, but mostly disbelief.

I was tired and happy when all 400 boxes were inside. They overflowed the dining room, which was hardly navigable anymore, spilling into the front hall on one side and the kitchen on the other. When Gary came home that night, his face just fell. To his credit, though, he didn't say anything. I showed him one, the proud owner of a bag with my own logo on it. He told me it was great and went into the den to watch football.

Besides the sale to Mary's cute little shop on Montana Avenue, I sold 400 bags to my friend Linda who owned a boutique in Manhattan. Also, through cold calling, I sold 600 bags to Oakville Grocery, a gourmet shop in Napa Valley. In all, 3000 bags were already sold by the time the order arrived. Not half, as I was hoping, but not bad either. By the end of 2005, a month later, I would sell through 4900 bags for a total of $4675, more than half of my first order. I would already be thinking about placing another order.

I dropped a thousand bags off at the dirty imprinter's shop the next week. When I came back to get them, he had done a good job of imprinting, but the bags were in a pile in a corner of his workshop, with bottom stiffeners strewn nearby. I stayed and folded each one by hand, putting the bottom stiffener back in carefully. He promised to do better the next time, but the next order was the same.

Within a few months, I would look again for a new screen printer. At least now I knew it could be done if you cure them on very low, low heat. When I found Nathan at Flannigan's in Van Nuys the next spring, an excellent screen printer with the professionalism to fold and box the bags, he didn't expect much from me. I would outperform his expectations, create another long-term friendship, and stick with him as my local printing vendor for a decade.

When I placed my first order with Amy, I did it without a tag for 1 Bag at a Time. I knew that I would have to cover the cost of printing them in Los Angeles and probably would have to tag the bags myself, but in September, that seemed like a theoretical issue. Now it was real. Along with grading papers, making dinner, and supervising homework, I was keeping track of orders and corresponding with Amy almost every night. On top of that, I needed to design a tag and create a website. I knew quite well that every bag was an advertisement, so the tag was important. I had found Amy from the tiny tag tucked inside The Essential Ingredient bag. If someone got one of my bags, I needed to make sure they knew where to get more. You never know where a bag will end up.

I had a lot of late nights that fall, often falling asleep well after midnight. It was a grueling schedule, up at 6 a.m., at work by 7:30. I don't really remember designing the tag, but I remember thinking about what to put on it. Obviously, my company name, logo, and website. Michael strongly encouraged me to put a picture of myself into brand materials. He said my personality would bring life to the newly birthed brand. I found a photo from a few years back, a simple image where I looked like an English teacher. I was willing to own that. Airborne, the immune supplement for air travelers, touted that it was created by a second-grade teacher. People trusted teachers, so I thought, *Maybe that will work for me.* I figured out how to convert the photo into black and white and put it on the tag. Then I wrote up a little blurb: The Perfect Re-Usable Bag for Groceries, Shopping, and Saving the World—1 Bag at a Time.

On the back of the tag, I put facts about plastic bag impacts that began to tell the story of bags:

Top 5 Reasons to Reuse a Bag:

- The petroleum in 14 plastic bags could drive a car 1 mile.
- Americans use over 14 billion bags annually.
- It takes 70% more global warming gasses to make a paper bag than a plastic bag.
- Paper bags do not biodegrade in landfills.
- Cities spend up to 17 cents per bag in disposal costs.

Those five facts, in slightly different versions, would remain on my tag over the next 12 years. As new statistics were published,

I would revise. The second fact changed the most. Statistics were hard to come by and I was finding that the statistics changed as science and interest in a topic changed. Later, it would read 380 billion bags, citing the EPA estimate.[21]

I decided that the tag should function like a cereal box. The front tries to call attention to what it is and why consumers might want to buy one. They too could save the world, 1 Bag at a Time. The information on the back won't sell the product, but it helps customers connect with the product after they buy it and makes them more likely to buy another one. I wrote the whole tag thinking about a consumer like me standing in a checkout line. It had to be appealing and make a compelling pitch for purchasing in a few seconds.

I decided that in my marketing, I would avoid negative words entirely, using only inspirational words that would help people want to do the right thing. I avoided saying anything negative about plastic bags. I talked about how our world could be cleaner with this one simple 99 cent solution. I would remain dedicated to positive language throughout my time as an entrepreneur. Words were important to me, and I used them carefully. Here is an image of that first tag. It's a pretty amateur tag, but it worked.

The
**PERFECT
RE-USABLE
BAG**
for groceries,
shopping, and
*SAVING
THE
WORLD–
1 BAG
AT A TIME!*™

With this bag, you can help save the world–1 bag at a time.™ Use it every time you shop for groceries and other purchases. Keep some in your car and discover how easy it is to preserve natural resources while you shop.
*Lisa Foster, Founder*

*TOP 5 REASONS
TO REUSE A BAG:*
1. The petroleum in 14 plastic bags could drive a car 1 mile.
2. Americans use over 14 billion plastic bags annually.
3. It takes 70% more global warming gasses to make a paper bag than a plastic bag.
4. Paper bags do not biodegrade in landfills.
5. Cities spend up to 17 cents per bag in disposal costs.

*RE-USE 1 BAG TODAY!*

www.1bagatatime.com
printed on recycled paper

6  89076 28313  7

Even that used a lot of skills that I didn't know I had. I'm not sure what software I used, but I think I used Microsoft Word, so the character spacing and fonts are primitive. It was also too big as a tag. It required a barcode. At $800, buying my own barcode prefix was one of the largest expense items from that first batch. Still, I'd been a consumer all my life, so it was easy to think like one. The tag wasn't all I designed that fall. I needed a website. One of the first drag-and-drop website platforms had just launched, called Homestead. Somewhere in the fog of the fall of 2005, I created an account and put up a website. The site looked a little bit like my tag, but the facts were fleshed out in an FAQ page with links to sources for the facts, and there was a whole page devoted to what I was calling the Perfect Re-Usable Grocery Bag. It was a badly designed site, but it did the trick for those first few months. Like my other early marketing efforts, it looked a little like an English teacher handout. But people liked it. I started to think that maybe I hadn't spent the last decade teaching persuasive writing for nothing.

By the time my bags arrived, all I needed was to put the tags on the bags. On Amazon I found those little plastic things that attach a tag to an article of goods and ordered some. Later, tags would be printed and affixed in China. Years later, when I visited the factory in China and saw a tableful of women dutifully tagging each bag before counting and boxing up orders, I felt a sympathy and gratitude that I'm sure they couldn't imagine surging through the heart of a Caucasian buyer.

At that moment, I needed to tag 2000 bags for Mary. It took me most of Thanksgiving weekend. Daryn and Kayla occasionally helped, but mostly, everyone watched football while I spent hours tagging each bag and re-boxing them in the dining room.

After Thanksgiving, I called Mary to let her know I would be delivering her bags. She said to drop them behind the store any time. I rented a cargo van, a beat-up old thing that totally dwarfed me, but it was roomy and strangely easy to drive. I backed it into the driveway and my girls helped me load ten boxes with 200 bags each inside. At some point, I cajoled them into helping me deliver the bags.

As we set out, it felt like an adventure. We were all giggling. I focused entirely on driving while the girls were trying to find some music on the tinny radio. After a few blocks, though, Daryn realized that someone might see her. By the time we started down Montana Avenue, a pretty stylish retail area in the heart of Santa Monica, Daryn and Kayla were both hiding under the dashboard to avoid being spotted in a delivery van. We pulled up to the back of the store, and the young woman there helped us unload. Mission accomplished. I had just delivered my first bag sale.

As I look back now, I see that my willingness to learn as I went was a huge asset. I didn't worry about getting things perfect and worked hard to control costs. I didn't have a separate bank account, so all the accounting was in a spreadsheet. I think Gary was surprised when I started putting money in the bank, which I did as soon as Mary paid, which was promptly. Often, I thought about Kim's brother, Peter Alexander, the Australian pajama king, for inspiration and felt lucky to be starting off in an age of search engines, websites, email, and cell phones. I really couldn't picture my mom taking an order on a yellow pad.

Every step of this first order was another opportunity to just keep going. I delivered orders and sent invoices for almost half a year, asking people to pay by check. In all that time, not a single person stiffed me. I figured if you are an early adopter of reusable grocery bags, you are not likely to be a deadbeat. I was increasingly convinced that the idea of reusable grocery bags was sticky, even in America.

I sort of fell in love with spreadsheets during this time. As an English teacher, my math skills were, well, let's just say underdeveloped. In school, I really loved math but was not encouraged, and I never went very far with it. Spreadsheets were liberating. I could set up all kinds of complex equations, and the calculations were done accurately and automatically. It was fantastic.

One of my first spreadsheets shows my early expenses, with totals for inventory, printing tags and the cost of the graphic artist, FedEx for a box of sample bags from China, the barcode fee, and some other expenses. After the order arrived, I spent an evening calculating the cubic meter of a carton and setting up the equation for estimating international shipping costs. Part of what I learned was that there would always be charges I couldn't know. Because of that, I always padded my cost estimates a little bit to account for surprises or hidden charges.

On the same spreadsheet, below the costs, I generated a list of pricing possibilities for 7500 bags. I have a note on the side: Keep 500 bags for promotion. I was pretty sure I would not make a profit on my first order, but I was also pretty sure I wouldn't lose any money, at least not much. So far, I was living up to my promise. For the next 12 years, I remained dedicated to being responsible about finances. Spreadsheets were invaluable in helping me achieve that. Even with my dedication to fiscal responsibility, I would later take a risk and nearly lose everything. But that would be much later.

Soon I was able to estimate the profit of any particular order. All I had to do was put in a proposed selling price and quantity into the spreadsheet and, automatically, calculations would adjust to show the weighted price of shipping and other expenses, and an estimated bottom line showing my profit. This was a beautiful thing. I could play with the price until I was reasonably sure that I would make a profit. As Michael said, it wasn't just a projection. It had to be based on reasonable assumptions. Because I wasn't in business to make a lot of money, I wasn't tempted by greed. I kept my pricing low. Later, as price wars started, I gained a reputation for being a tough competitor and won large contracts by being disciplined about profit margins.

I was grateful for, and amazed at, all this new technology. Here I was, an English teacher, selling a product that I'd found in Australia, sourced from China, into markets across the US with just a computer, a mobile phone, and a website. Even five years earlier, this would have been, if not impossible, much harder.

Anyway, according to my first spreadsheet devoted to orders, I sold through my entire first order of 8000 bags by May of 2006. Knowing that it took some three months to get inventory, I ordered 8000 more sometime in February or March.

I was also thinking about super-connectors. The tag spread the message. The product enabled new behavior. Now I needed people who could help me get the message out to a wider audience.

Sometime that fall, one of my friends introduced me to Dean Kubani, who worked in sustainability for the City of Santa Monica. He was kind enough to set up a lunch. As I recall, I had difficulty connecting with Dean. I'm pretty sure I was off my game. I didn't yet know how to come prepared for this kind of meeting. Certainly, I came in less prepared than I should have been. Also, I was just beginning to have a vision disorder that drew my eyes involuntarily to the right, and that was a distraction. He kept looking over his shoulder following my gaze, but I couldn't control it. Anyway, I told him what I was doing. I didn't really mean to pitch him, but I slipped into my story and pitch. Dean heard me out, though he was a little skeptical. Obviously, I had a vested interest in selling bags, and he didn't want the government to be used to the benefit of industry. It wasn't my best meeting, but I managed to pique his interest in the topic. Santa Monica soon after began to investigate the issue of plastic bags and was one of the first cities to implement a bag ban.

Knowing that Martha's Vineyard, like vacation spots everywhere, draws visitors from all over the US, it was a natural for me to call up my favorite natural grocery store there,

Cronig's. Run by Steve Bernier, a business leader who had been dedicated to customer service and environmental responsibility for years, Cronig's is an Island institution. Steve never offered plastic grocery bags. He was aware of the environmental impacts of plastic, and as an Islander, he wanted no plastic bag with his store name to blow accidentally into the ocean. The store offered paper bags only.

I called him about March of 2006 and gave him my pitch. I told him I was a long-time visitor and homeowner on the Island, which I think gave me some credibility. I explained the impacts of plastic bags and ended with: I have a product that will help solve this problem for 99 cents. It's made from a new, technological fabric that is machine washable and designed to last up to a year. Imagine, a grocery bag that creates zero waste for a year!

I had made this pitch dozens of times, and usually the manager had questions and wanted to get more information. Steve was different. He was quiet for a minute and said, I know perfectly well the disaster that plastic bags are creating, and that's why I've never offered them. But paper bags are breaking my bank. They cost me seven cents each and I have to give them away to compete. Maybe this is the solution I need. You say people will pay for this bag?

I told him about Ireland and Australia. We discussed marketing for a while. I said I would work to get an article in our local newspaper explaining bag impacts and why reusable bags are better. It was a feel-good story, and I was pretty sure I could pitch it. I also told him about my first encounter with reusable bags in Australia, with bags right at the checkout stand. I told him that in Australia, the cashier didn't ask, Paper or plastic? but instead asked, Would you like a bag? Did he think his cashiers would change the question at checkout?

Let me think about it, he said. In any case, I'll find a spot near checkout for them.

Then we discussed the logo. Steve was clear: If it's a grocery bag, it has our name on it. It occurred to me that for store owners, the one thing that single-use bags and reusable bags shared was their logo. That was the mythical idea that I could graft onto this new idea to make it acceptable to established grocers. I told him he would have to take 8000 bags to do that. He didn't hesitate.

When I sold my first order of fully imprinted bags to Steve Bernier that April, I didn't realize it then, but I was in the beginning of what would become a hockey-stick growth curve. It's a growth curve that rises and then, like a hockey stick, takes a sharp turn upward as growth explodes exponentially. I placed my first order of 8000 bags in August 2005. The following March, I ordered another 8000 for me and 8000 for Cronig's, doubling my order rate. I would order more than 30,000 bags in the next few months, before mid-summer, doubling my order rate again in half the time. By the end of the year, I would be placing purchase orders for 100,000 bags. It was the beginning of a wild ride. Pretty soon customers would be calling me, and I would be taking orders as fast as I could write them. I'm getting ahead of myself now. Still, even as early as the spring of 2006, I felt things begin to accelerate.

## Chapter 6

# Cold Calling and Conventions

As we entered early 2006, I was still working to find anyone who could possibly be a super-connector. I started reaching out via networking to anyone I knew and cold calling anyone I wanted to know.

My geographic reach started to expand. One discovery I made was my love of calling stores in the South. No one bought my bags there, but everyone was so polite that it was a pleasure to talk to them. The receptionists were often chatty and willing to pass the call along to a buyer who was just as polite and chatty. Even when they decided not to buy my bags, their refusals were eminently pleasant.

Well, now, this is certainly a lovely bag, and I can see that it would do a great job. We just don't think our customers are quite ready to purchase a 99 cent bag right now. We work hard to make sure things are affordable for our customers, but I will keep this around and keep you in mind.

I made a mental note that I was more likely to get someone to engage in a conversation about bags if we spent a few minutes connecting before getting down to business. I also noted that difficult conversations were easier if I remained cheerful and polite even when broaching the tougher parts of the call. These tactics sharpened my sales edge.

In sales, being able to connect and be pleasant are essential skills. Talking to people in the South upped my game. I learned how to say no without ever saying no. I made a habit of having a little chat with everyone at the start of the

> *I learned how to say no without ever saying no.*

call. I checked the weather for the area I was calling before I picked up the phone, and made a note to ask about snow, or heat, or if they were anywhere near the flood that I'd seen on the news last week. When people asked me about my weather, I would always give a little laugh and say, You know, in Los Angeles, the weather is boring. We don't complain about weather here, we complain about traffic.

No one likes to hear that you have better weather than they do, so shifting to traffic gave the customer that upper edge. They would always start talking about how they didn't have any trouble with traffic, not like LA, and they could feel better about where they were. That was a good point in the conversation to ask if they'd received the sample bag I sent.

I quickly got bold in cold calling as I polished my pitch. I applied exactly what I learned from small stores to ever larger stores. Sometime in the early months of 2006, I targeted Safeway. I called the receptionist, chatted a bit, and explained I was a vendor with a new grocery bag product. Could she connect me to the grocery bag buyer? It took some persistence because usually the receptionist had no idea who was responsible for buying grocery bags. I was very understanding and patient and kept my sense of humor. In the nicest way possible, I didn't take no for an answer and always worked to find a way through.

Surprisingly, Safeway was very open to vendors with new products, and it didn't take me long to get the grocery bag buyer for the western US on the line. She listened to my pitch, and then, without hesitation said: Our research indicates that fewer than 3% of Americans use reusable bags. That number has not changed since the 1970s and we don't expect it to change now. Good luck.

At least she listened and stated her reasons. Though she passed, I felt a lot of respect for her.

It was different for Trader Joe's. No matter what I did, I ran into a wall. The buyer was out. Did I want to leave another message? I finally got an address and sent him a sales kit. When

I called to follow-up, he again refused to pick up my calls. There was nothing I could say or do to get the smallest response at all. A few months later, I noticed my local Trader Joe's was promoting reusable bags. If you reused a bag, the cashier gave you a little slip of paper to fill out with your name and number, and you could drop it into a jar. Each store was giving out a $25 gift card to one lucky customer that week who reused a bag. Within a year, they would be sourcing their own bags.

I have to admit, I felt burned. I totally respected their right to source directly and to say no. What made me angry was they didn't have the courtesy to pick up the phone. Later, as my company grew, I would get random phone calls from other entrepreneurs or salespeople and I always took the call, even from people I had no interest in. It was about being a professional and being a decent human being.

Another connection I made in early 2006 was the one that would be most valuable. It was Jeffrey Hollender, then CEO of Seventh Generation. The previous December, I'd received a fundraising call from Putney School, and I shared my new bag adventure with the advancement person, who told me that Jeffrey had gone to Putney. The school is a tiny community and he offered to connect me. I looked Jeffrey up and was impressed. His focus was clearly on business being a positive force for humanity.

As I was embarking on my own business, Jeffrey became a great role model. You can be successful while selling responsible products and taking care of people along your supply chain. I sent Jeffrey an email in January of 2006. His assistant set up a time to call. On a chilly January day, as I stood overlooking the faculty parking lot at Harvard-Westlake, we connected.

Jeffrey and I chatted about Putney for a bit, both of us having fond memories there. Then he asked me to tell him what I was doing. I recited my bag facts and ended with the advantages of my bags. I was careful not to pitch him. At the end, I told him

I admired the success he'd achieved through being dedicated to the environment and people, even as he grew a thriving business. I was just reaching out for any advice or thoughts he might have.

He said: I think you'll be very successful. Tell you what, why don't I give you a badge for Expo West in March? You can come see what the natural food industry looks like, and I'd be happy to meet you.

My heart expanded a little bit when he said I'd be successful. There was that drug again, someone with an expectation of my success. When someone else believes in you, it's a lot easier to believe in yourself. I accepted his offer. Later that evening, I spent a lot of time on the website learning that Expo West was the largest natural food and natural product convention in the US. This turned out to be a whole new tipping point for me.

If I wanted to learn how to think like a vendor, there was no better place than Expo West. It's hosted at the Anaheim Convention Center, about an hour south of Los Angeles on a good day. A larger-than-life presentation of everything in the natural grocery industry, it's the central buying and selling marketplace for natural products new and old. Think about a Whole Foods store, then blow up every brand of corn chips, recycled plastic toothbrushes, and everything else into a booth for selling. Small brands have small booths. Large brands mount enormous kiosks, specially constructed with themes and amenities. Amy's Frozen Foods occupied a whole aisle with delicious foods heated and ready to sample. Seventh Generation created a giant display with a tropical theme and palm trees.

When Jeffrey's assistant mailed me the link to register for a Seventh Generation badge the next week, I was able to start figuring out what the show offered. There were lists of vendors, pages of maps, and catalogs of talks and networking events. There was no way to do it all. I would need a plan. While it was easy to find organic pet food or vegan pizza brands, the store representatives that I wanted to meet would be walking around from booth to booth. They were everywhere, but there was no central place to find them. I would have to be clever about networking and introducing myself to total strangers. As I browsed the catalog of events, one opportunity caught my attention. It was a chance to pitch a new product to a panel of natural food editors with a possibility of being included in press coverage. I would later learn that brands could buy time with editors and make sure their press kits were seen. This seemed as good a shot as I was going to get to attract media coverage. It was a two-hour event, starting with a moderated panel of editors and PR agents about how to pitch your product, and then a chance at an open mic to pitch.

At an event as big as Expo West, with major brands making huge investments in becoming the next big thing (that year, it was coconut water), it takes a lot to break through. If I could get journalists to resonate with my tragic story of plastic bags and the advantages of reusable bags, maybe I could get some coverage. I started to think about what journalists need. They need a lede. They need something that's new and a clear reason why it's compelling. I reworked my pitch as a media article and wrote out an outline for the facts I wanted to include. Again, my background as an English teacher and my years of teaching persuasive writing came in handy.

Expo West is a three-day event, Friday through Sunday. The media panel was on Friday afternoon from 4 to 6 p.m. There were two days afterwards that I could make use of. I bought a little wheeled file cabinet from Staples where I could stash about 50 sample bags and some flyers. I tagged about 200 bags that I expected to give away. My mantra would be: Every bag is an advertisement. Just get them out there. I revised my sales sheet and got some business cards printed up. The sales sheet still looked like an English teacher handout—too many words, not enough images. I'm a little embarrassed to say that it didn't have an image at all. I used what I knew, and what I knew was words. Having a sample bag was better than images anyway. I was confident that I could be charming and persuasive and hoped that would be enough.

Even though vendors weren't my main target audience, I thought maybe they would want a branded bag of their own. I started preparing a pitch aimed at vendors like me who wanted attention from natural grocery store buyers.

A week before the event, I was ready. I had three goals:

1. Get to the media pitching event on Friday and make a pitch.
2. On Saturday and Sunday, wander the aisles and pitch to vendors, introducing myself to any random buyers I could manage to connect with.
3. Meet with Jeffrey Hollender in person. We scheduled a meet-and-greet on Sunday.

I worked on my media and vendor pitches, so I had them down before the event. I printed up a stack of 200 sales sheets. I was sure it would be too many, but better too many than too few.

For Friday, the schedule would be tight. My last class ended at 2 p.m. The pitching event started at four and ended at six. I would have two hours to get to Anaheim from the Valley, about 35 miles. With Friday traffic conditions, I wasn't sure I could do it. I hoped that 2 p.m. would be early enough to beat the worst of it.

One thing you learn not to do in Los Angeles is underestimate traffic. My car was ready to go with my wheeled case stuffed with bags and a stack of sales sheets. As soon as my class ended, I dashed to my desk, grabbed my stuff, and got on the freeway. Of course, it was already jammed. After about an hour in traffic, my stress level started going up as I realized how late I would be. Sometimes going 10 miles an hour, sometimes entirely at a standstill, I realized that I might miss the media event entirely. I wanted desperately to make it, but Los Angeles traffic doesn't really care about how important it is to be anywhere. I inched along, getting more agitated by the minute. About 5 miles away from the convention center, dusk was falling. It was nearly 5 p.m. and I'd been driving for three hours. I'd already missed the first half of the event as I crawled toward the freeway exit. I still had to park and find the event space. Even if I got to the open mic, I would probably make all the mistakes they had just spent an hour telling you not to make. I had a bad feeling about the whole thing, but I'd worked too hard to give up. Besides, I wasn't a quitter, and even in the face of long odds, I knew I needed to keep going. No matter how late, no matter how many mistakes, I would step up to the mic.

That's when my entire car dashboard lit up in yellow with a black exclamation point in the middle. System failure. This was the little blue Prius that I'd bought shortly before I went to Australia. Somehow, at the worst possible moment, the motor had a catastrophic failure. For those last couple of miles, I was grateful that traffic wasn't going faster than 10 miles an hour. I was on battery power, so I had all the speed of a golf cart. I coasted off the freeway at the convention center exit, praying that the electric motor would hang on. I got to the parking garage and paid the outrageous parking fee (they were charging by the day, even though I was arriving for the last hour). I coasted to a spot near an entrance that I hoped wasn't too far from the pitching event. Parking-wise, I was lucky to be so late. People were already leaving and there were plenty of spots available. When I turned my car off, I was pretty sure it wouldn't start up again to get me home, but I would deal with it later. Grabbing my stuff, I set off as fast as I could.

They were just at the point I feared. The moderator was wrapping up the panel discussion, thanking the panelists and inviting people up to the mic. I found a spot in back to catch my breath. My heart was pounding. The stress of the traffic jam, car failure, and being late gripped my body, along with the stress of a high-stakes pitch that I suspected I would blow fantastically. I let a few others pitch first, trying to listen and pick up on any tips I might have missed. Honestly, I couldn't hear a word. All I could hear was the blood in my ears.

Somewhere under all that stress, there was still that fire in my heart. Every time I wonder where I got the courage to do something, I can feel the expectation that I wouldn't do much deep inside me, giving me the freedom to fail and, also, offering me the opportunity to overperform. This is what I had come for. After one or two pitches, I ignored the blood pounding and got in line to pitch.

I have no idea what I said when I stepped up to the mic. It was something like the pitch I gave store managers, I think. I tried to tell the tragic story of a plastic bag and tout the advantages of this new bag, and I held one up. I'm pretty sure I said something about this being the number-one selling bag in Australia. The whole time I was speaking, a powerful wave of stress swept over me, and I had very little ability to control what I said, thought, did, or remembered. I think it was a panic attack, which I am not prone to. When I ended, the whole room was looking at me. I tried to regain composure.

Now, there's no reason to be nervous here, the moderator started telling me.

Clearly, I had hyperventilated through my pitch, and now embarrassment started to set in. I wanted to tell them my car had just died, that I'd been in traffic for three hours, that my English class ended at 2 p.m. in the Valley, and I couldn't have been here any earlier. But I knew these would sound like excuses. I said nothing, tried to smile, and did my best to slow my breathing down.

Who are you pitching to? she asked. She tried to make her voice sound kind, but sure enough, I knew that I'd violated the first rule of pitching, naming the panelist you were targeting. I had no idea who they were. A sign near the stage listed the panelists, so I read aloud the first one I saw. There was no time to process them.

The woman whose name I mentioned leaned forward to her mic. Sorry, I don't think this story is for me.

I took a beat. It was a failure, but I knew that everything about what I was doing was a long shot. It certainly wasn't going to come easy. I felt like my car. I should have paid attention to the big yellow light with the exclamation point in it. It was telling me something. I gathered my stuff to walk away.

As I turned away from the mic, I heard another voice from the stage. A different journalist leaned forward and said: Come and give me your card before you leave.

I can't think of another time in my life when I bounced from rock bottom to the top of the world so quickly. I'm not sure I can describe how I felt. I knew at that moment, in spite of everything against me, the pitch had landed. The traffic, the stress, the panic attack and hyperventilating had all been worth it. In my head, I mentally marked my tipping-point strategy inner map. That journalist, who invited me to contact him, would be my first real super-connector. I felt enormous gratitude to him for speaking up, even though I hadn't chosen him. I returned to my chair at the back. My blood was still pounding, but instead of dread, it signaled success.

I had not yet caught my breath when a young woman from a nearby seat came and sat next to me. She was a purchasing manager from a natural food store in Maine. Could she have a bag and a card? We exchanged information, and I put her card in my pocket with a note to contact her after the show. When she went back to her seat, another store manager was waiting to meet me. I had a dozen business cards in my pocket when the event was over, including the card of the journalist who wanted more information. I told him about my car dying and we had a good laugh about what a wreck I'd been as I stepped up to the mic.

As we chatted, I told him: I really believe this product will be as successful here as it has been in Australia and Ireland. Its time has come in the US. Thanks so much for your interest.

You had a lot of nerve to make that pitch under the circumstances, he said, but in spite of your nervousness, there was something in your pitch. I think you're tapping into something big for this audience. Email me info right away.

He took a sample bag but refused any other materials, showing me a stack of plastic bags behind his chair overflowing with press kits and samples. He had enough to carry. I sent him follow-up information by Sunday night. By the time he published, he wasn't the only one spreading the message of reusable bags. Over the next two days, I would see my message amplified in places that were entirely unexpected.

It was well after seven and dark when I walked out to my car. I called AAA for a jump start and hoped I would get home. I called Gary and told him I'd be late, explained about the car and the pitch. He told me to find a hotel room and not get on the freeway, but I didn't have clothes for the next morning and would need more sample bags. If I could get the car started, I'd come home. I'd have to take his car the next morning and he'd have to deal with mine. He was okay with that. I think he was a little afraid of me getting in a car in my state of mind, so he did his best to calm me down. He knew full well that the car failure was no match for my happiness at having landed my pitch and attracting customers too.

It took less than an hour to breeze home, all traffic having magically disappeared. I was in Anaheim, home of the Magic Kingdom, the happiest place on earth.

Saturday was my first full day of the Expo West experience. I left Los Angeles at 8 a.m. and cruised into Anaheim about 45 minutes later—no traffic at all on a weekend morning. The parking fee was again outrageous, but this time, it felt like an investment. I had a few minutes before the doors opened officially at nine, so I sat down where people were starting to show up. I took a minute to breathe the Southern California air—72 degrees (22C) and sunny even in early March.

Just before the doors opened, I met The Bag Monster. The Bag Monster is a publicity stunt dreamed up by Andy Keller, founder of Chico Bag, maker of reusable bags that sell for $5 to $13 each. I would come to know and admire Andy later. About the time I learned of the impacts of plastic grocery bags on the environment, Andy learned of them too. His solution was a nylon bag that tucked neatly into a little stuff bag. He offered a few colors, and his website was much slicker than mine. He had raised enough money to set up manufacturing in California, which to me was an incredible feat. They were an upscale bag, not a mass-market bag the way my bag was. Andy had a glint in his eye that I liked. Even covered in a suit of old plastic bags, I could see he had an energy about him that would carry him through a lot. He would need it.

He bounced right up to me and said: Hi! I'm The Bag Monster. This outfit is made with five hundred and ten bags, the number of bags one person throws away every year. Have you ever thought about how many bags you use? Most people use about ten bags a week, or five hundred and ten a year. This is what that looks like.

I told him that, yes, actually I did think about how many bags I used, quite a bit in fact. I introduced myself and showed him my sample bags. Spontaneously, we had both started bag companies at nearly the exact same time, and both found ourselves at Expo West. Andy, over 6 feet tall and clad in plastic bags, was more visible than I was. Immediately, we recognized in each other a kindred spirit.

Five years later, when plastic bag bans started cropping up, Andy was the guy the plastic bag industry sued as they tried to hang on to their market share. *Rolling Stone* magazine[22] would accuse the plastic industry of using every bullying tactic the tobacco industry had used. All that would come later. Right now, we both took heart that there was another person motivated by the waste of plastic bags and doing something to change it in the US. We felt we were on the leading edge of something, and we hoped the wave would be big enough to float both our boats.

In total, Expo West is about the area of three city blocks if you include the ancillary hall for manufacturing products, and the basement where new brands and bargain hunters purchase cheaper booths. That's where I would be the next year, in the basement. But in 2006, I walked up and down the aisles, talking to anyone who would listen to my tragic story of the plastic bag and get a sample of the mythical new, reusable bag that makes no waste for up to a year. I was surrounded by my target audience. More than once, I would approach a vendor and find myself with a few other attendees listening with interest to the story. Often, they identified themselves as buyers and would give me their cards. Vendors saw the idea stick and, reluctantly, would give me their cards too.

Several times that morning, I went out to my car to get more sample bags and sales sheets. Sometime after lunch, I ran out of sales sheets and found a FedEx Office conveniently located in the basement of the building. I'd presciently put a copy of it on a little memory stick and was able to print up a few hundred more onsite and went back up to roam the halls again. By the end of the day, the bank of foot massage stations at the front of the hall was filled and I wished for an extra ten minutes and twenty bucks for a massage, but I just went home. It was after six when the doors closed. I had a long drive and another long day ahead.

On Sunday, I met with Jeffrey Hollender at the Seventh Generation kiosk. It was a huge display that looked like a big yellow tree house. As I recall, there were palm trees outside and suspension bridges between a couple of raised indoor spaces for meetings and product displays. Many stores contract for annual purchases at Expo West, so there was plenty of space for buyers to connect with a friendly salesperson.

Jeffrey couldn't have been nicer. I told him about being a wreck on Friday evening but still landing my pitch. I told him Saturday was great wandering the aisles and meeting plenty of people willing to listen. I thanked him profusely for sponsoring my badge. I asked about what his goals were and who he most looked forward to connecting with. There was little he could offer me at that point, and little that I needed. I was happy to have met him and I would reach out occasionally over the next few years to keep him abreast of how I was doing. He was always kind and encouraging, which was all I needed.

Sunday played out like Saturday until sometime in the early afternoon. I was standing with a vendor, giving my pitch, when I heard an announcement on the loudspeaker: Attention, attendees! Expo West will be limiting the number of plastic bags allowed for each attendee. Please take no more than seven plastic bags as you leave. I repeat, attendees will be allowed no more than seven plastic bags per person.

It was another tipping point. The whole event was a super-duper-connector event and my message (and Andy's) had stuck at the highest level of the convention. It's hard to describe what I felt, but any early doubts I'd had—the lingering effects of the doubters who turned me down, told me not to do it, said it couldn't happen in America—vanished. The message was sticky. Later, whole organizations would emerge to pick up the message about the unnecessary and devastating waste that single-use plastics were wreaking on our environment. The Plastic Pollution Coalition and others would be inspired by these early messages and dedicate themselves to fighting and solving the problems. My strategy was working, at least inside the halls of Expo West, which indicated that the natural products industry was on board. The only thing left to wonder was, when would the rest of America be ready to accept this message?

## Chapter 7

# Hit Your Tipping Point

Not long after Expo West 2006, I was driving home from work when my cell phone rang. I picked it up and it was a guy named Bill from a conservation organization called The Last Green Valley in Connecticut. He wanted to place an order. I had been cold calling for some eight months and now, for the first time, someone was calling me.

For me the spring of 2006 turned out to be not just a tipping point, but The Tipping Point, the moment when I entered a hockey-stick growth curve that transformed my business from a side-gig to a real business bringing in millions of dollars in revenue. It wasn't just me, though.

The third part of Gladwell's *Tipping Point* formula is context, and it was no accident that my business took off just as the whole country seemed to tip into the new century, even if ever so slightly. Just as we had collective amnesia about the environmental disaster that we knew plastic grocery bags would be, we forgot about other ways that our daily choices were having a devastating impact on the environment. Big agriculture increasingly depended on chemicals and machines to squeeze costs down and maximize food production. Beautiful, oversized apples and chickens were cheap and plentiful. Genetically modified organisms (GMOs) showed up in foodstuffs on grocery shelves for prices that Americans on the low end of the income inequality scale could buy. To be sure, food accessibility is a good thing, but by 2005, studies estimated that about one third of the food that Americans bought ended up in the trash bin. As with plastic bags, we hardly noticed all that waste.

The same years saw the rise of Whole Foods, Seventh Generation, and the organic movement, a response to what was appearing at mainstream grocery stores. Some people didn't trust highly processed foods, chemicals, and additives, not to mention GMOs. It got to the point where you either ate organic kale for lunch or you made fun of people who ate organic kale for lunch. As the idea of trust in public life began to slip away for many people, some brands doubled down on being trustworthy and earned a loyal following.

I'd been a natural food shopper since long before we went to Australia. Still, it wasn't until I came back from down under that I noticed plastic bags floating above the roadways of Los Angeles. Once I did notice them, not a single day went by when I didn't see one, often two or three. Sometimes they blew up right to my doorstep as if they were talking to me, maybe shouting.

In contrast to Australia, the American lifestyle suddenly seemed excessive to me, a lifestyle, if not rich and famous, then prone to incredible waste. Didn't it make more sense to produce less food and eat what we grow instead of putting a third of it in landfill? Didn't it make more sense to have a few bags that you use for a year than to throw bags away at a rate that was hard to fathom?

It felt to me like we were collectively taking the nozzle at the gas pump, putting it in the trash can, letting it flow—and then paying the bill. Why were we raising our $CO_2$ levels and endangering our habitat for products we were throwing away? The year before, I had felt as though I was one of a small subset of Americans who thought about those questions. In 2006 after *An Inconvenient Truth*, a lot of other people were starting to ask too.

*An Inconvenient Truth* came out in May 2006. It was produced by my friend Laurie David, the one who told me: That bag thing, you should do it. When we walked a year earlier on Martha's Vineyard, I didn't know she was already in production with Al Gore. His documentary reconnected our lives to the world around us. In my tipping-point strategy, this was the context that I needed. Acceptance of climate change was moving toward the mainstream, and it would pull reusable bags into the realm of normalcy.

To be sure, I knew that those ubiquitous, flimsy plastic bags contributed only a tiny fraction to the global damage of fossil fuel or plastic waste. The 12 million barrels of oil consumed in making bags represented just 0.3% of the estimated 36 billion barrels of oil consumed annually on a worldwide basis. Still, the $CO_2$ burned for every bag ever made still hangs somewhere in our atmosphere, and the physical bag still lies somewhere in a landfill, or as tiny bits in the ocean, or drifting about somewhere in between. The visibility of disposable plastic bags was compelling to me, used for 10 or 20 minutes and discarded forever. They were a symbol of our throwaway society, and, as an English teacher, I was attuned to the power of symbols.

By the time Gore's documentary came out, my website was up and running and my supply chain was well established. I had been cold calling for months, and now, customers were calling me. I started getting media recognition after Expo West and spent most of March and April following up on leads gathered at the convention.

My family was used to having boxes in the dining room as a more-or-less permanent fixture. I was still teaching, but it was increasingly clear that bags were no longer a hobby but a full-time job. Every free period I had at school was spent calling potential customers and arranging logistics. Every evening after dinner, I would write purchase orders, print order confirmations, invoices, packing slips and labels, and box up bags to ship the next day. This often went late into the night.

One day, I was on my way to purchase more boxes when my phone rang. It was a representative from FedEx.

I notice that you're shipping more than usual, she said. I'm just calling to see what's going on and if there is anything that I can do to lower your shipping rate.

Shipping costs were killing me. I started passing them on to customers, which had become difficult to navigate during the sales process. I would love for her to lower my rate! I told her about the impacts of bags on the environment and that I was selling a new reusable bag that made no waste for up to a year. She promised to lower my rate and asked if I could send her a couple of my bags. A week later, my shipping rate went down, and she received her bags.

The bags from Amy came in boxes of 200, and most stores wanted 100 to start, so there was a lot of re-boxing. Later I would negotiate with Amy to send them in smaller cartons. I was also putting together sales and media kits, which also needed boxes. Random requests from women here and there for ten bags at a time kept arriving in my inbox and I often wasn't sure how they found me. That was a good sign, I figured. My message was out there, maybe in a small way, but it was there, and people were responding.

When random consumers called or emailed, I took their information and put ten bags and an invoice inside a box, telling them to send a check when they received it. And they did. There was only one woman I had trouble collecting from. She hadn't paid after several months and numerous reminders from me. I never asked for a late fee, never let my tone turn negative. I was determined to be positive in every interaction, so I sent a friendly reminder every couple of weeks.

Finally, she emailed me saying she had been in a car accident and was behind on bills but wasn't a deadbeat. My heart sank a little. I'm sure if I had been on the phone, I would have told her to take the bags as a gift. I can't remember how I replied, but sure enough, her check for ten dollars arrived a couple of weeks later. I thanked her profusely. I was learning collection skills, which required as much patience and politeness as selling. These small sales were hardly worth it financially, but I kept thinking, *Every bag is an advertisement, and you never know who will end up with it.*

I always told my kids there is a hard way and an easy way

to learn anything. Later, as cash flow tightened and more was at stake, I learned the hard way what happens when you're too hard on customers. The one and only time I imposed a late fee, I lost the customer. It was

*There is a hard way and an easy way to learn anything.*

a large customer too. It would take me some time to figure out how to be tough on issues, particularly what they owed me, while staying soft and understanding with people, working with them to find ways to make it possible for them to pay.

The sound of tape reverberated through the house at night, often past midnight. I was as tired as anyone else. Eventually, Gary said that if I couldn't have more reasonable hours, I would have to hire help. I said I would work on it.

The first thing I needed to do was quit my job. As much as I loved teaching, if I was going to have a shot at making it at all in this business, I would need to give it my full attention. Gary was supportive. Next, I had to discuss it with my kids.

Daryn and Kayla were certainly aware that I was selling bags and were often conscripted as my accomplices. But when I told them that I was going to quit teaching to devote myself full-time to selling grocery bags, they were visibly shocked. In their minds, their mom was an English teacher. It would take them some time to accept my new profession.

I would find later that many of my friends would be hard-pressed to let go of their idea of me as an English teacher and book-club leader. My mother, who never accepted that I worked outside the home, would call me up on random weekdays and ask me what I was doing. She had no idea what the world of work was, and so could not understand why I wouldn't always be available on a Tuesday morning to chat idly about manicures or the dog.

I began to see the stickiness of identity. Like expectation, it's a hidden force that keeps us in patterns that limit our success.

I knew I would always evoke a mixture of admiration and disbelief (but mostly disbelief) in people who could not accept me hauling 40-pound boxes, showing up at freight docks, wiring hundreds of thousands of dollars to China, overcoming obstacles, and doing everything except quit and go back to being an English teacher, which is what people expected of me. If other people couldn't adjust their idea of who I was becoming and what I could do, there was little I could do about that. What I refused to do any longer was let their expectations hold me back. In the end, my kids became even prouder of their entrepreneurial mom than they had been of their teacher mom.

After letting my family know that I was leaving teaching, I now had to tell my boss. Sometime in April, I asked the head of my department if I could speak to him privately. We found an empty classroom and I closed the door. Of course, I started with a story, that I had found reusable bags when I was in Australia, decided to take on reducing bag waste in the US as a moral imperative, discovered the tragic facts of plastic bags and the miraculous new reusable bag. I told him that I loved teaching, but I thought I could have an even bigger and more positive impact on the world if I devoted myself to this cause.

He listened with interest at first. When I ended, he had a strange smile on his face. Oddly, there was no trace of disbelief at all.

He asked, Can I invest?

If anyone knew my work ethic, it was my department head. I was encouraged by his belief in me, but I wasn't ready to take on an investor. I wasn't sure I'd make any money at this, and I didn't want to be indebted for a promise I couldn't keep. I declined as politely as I could and promised him a couple of sample bags. He said he would talk to HR and find out what else I had to do. Quitting, which was not something I did often, was easier than I thought.

Sometime in May, as I was finishing my classes, my department head notified me that the headmaster wanted to see me regarding my departure. I set up a time to meet with Tom Hudnut, our head of school. Tom is legendary, tall, and imposing, a power broker among power brokers. He was said to inspire awe and fear even in Hollywood where awe and fear are abundant. Among faculty, he was mostly feared. It was rumored that teachers who made the slightest hint of criticism or disloyalty were summarily fired, with Tom saying, Don't let the door hit you on the way out. Although I'm not easily daunted, I was terrified to go in there and announce I was quitting.

My fears were unfounded. Tom was eminently gracious. What's this I hear you're doing? he asked as he invited me into his office. He had known about my semester in Australia, of course. In this meeting, though, he seemed singularly focused on the bag business I was building. So, I gave him my pitch. Tom listened attentively and sat for a minute thoughtfully.

Well, I wish you much success, he said, and then added, When you're ready for Ralph's, let me know. One of the members on the board of Ralph's is on my board.

Walking out of his office, I recognized that Tom was a super-connector. Rather than hitting me with the door on the way out, he was opening a door for me. Ralph's is the dominant grocery chain in Southern California with hundreds of stores in the region. No one easily said no to Tom, and I knew how powerful it would be for Tom to give a sales kit from me directly to a board member of Ralph's.

I spent days composing a cover letter to Robert Beyer. I did some research on him, found he had been in investment banking and worked closely with Ron Berkle, a powerhouse in the grocery industry. I thought long and hard about what would be important to a couple of guys like that. Profits, certainly, but also, like the buyer at Safeway, giving customers what they wanted at a price they could afford. The strategy I went with was an argument about how 1 Bag at a Time could benefit Ralph's.

Here's a copy of the letter I finally composed:

May 31, 2006

Dear Mr. Beyer

Thank you for taking a moment to consider selling reusable bags at Ralph's. As the hurricane season begins and gas prices rise, a growing number of Americans are beginning to question business as usual. Some see the prospect of global warming as cause for depression, but I see it as the most exciting business opportunity in a generation.

Let me first acquaint you with the often unseen costs of single-use bags:

* There is enough petroleum in 14 plastic bags to drive a car one mile.
* Americans consume 14 billion plastic bags per year.
* Making a paper bag emits 70% more global warming gasses and 50 times more water pollution than making a plastic bag.
* Paper bags do not biodegrade in landfills, where 80% end up.
* In 1999, Americans used 10 billion paper shopping bags, consuming 14 million trees.
* San Francisco estimates that disposal of paper and plastic bags costs 17 cents a bag.
* NYC estimates that if each resident reduced shopping bag use by one bag a year, the city would save $250,000.

Many countries have responded to these facts by encouraging reusable bags through taxes or voluntary campaigns. The bag I am selling is fast becoming the most popular bag in the world. It beats disposable bags handily: it is bigger, easier to handle and carry, cleaner and lighter than other reusable alternatives, and it is affordable and attractive to boot.

As you know, bags are a significant expense for retail markets. This bag, which retails from 99 cents to $1.99, reduces that expense. Even markets that sell them at cost, as many do around the world, improve their bottom line while simultaneously generating positive corporate image.

These bags are a win-win for everyone. Please consider the attached proposal to introduce Ralph's customers to this product. I look forward to hearing from you.

Along with the letter, I had a 14-page proposal for how to pilot, market, and promote reusable bags, along with my little price list and several pages of bag facts with charts and references to the Australian report. As I look back on it, the cover letter wasn't bad for a rookie. But I shiver a little when I think about the whole package. It was a little presumptuous of me to offer marketing advice to them. There were too many pages, no images, and it still looked too much like an English teacher handout. I left the packet with a few sample bags on Tom Hudnut's desk a couple of days later. Leaving, I held my breath. I kept telling myself, *You just never know, you just never know.*

In my last weeks of teaching, I felt so many emotions it's hard to capture them all. I loved being with bright, motivated students, challenging them and being challenged by them, joking around, inspiring them, watching as they realized that

*You just never know, you just never know.*

the characters we talked about had many of the same concerns and problems they had. There was much I would miss.

On the whole, though, what I felt most was my delight in selling reusable grocery bags, my commitment to changing the way America shopped, and my excitement about the strange new world of business. I was fully convinced that reusable bags were a win-win-win product, good for consumers, good for businesses, and good for the environment. After Expo West and

*An Inconvenient Truth*, I felt that the timing couldn't be better. My students immediately shared my excitement and enthusiasm. I brought bags to school for students who wanted them. Teachers too wanted a bag, so friends from the history department and the French department started coming down to visit my desk. No longer relegated to the back staircase, I was now selling bags right out of the English Department office. At our end-of-year traditional faculty picnic, Tom gave me a fond farewell among the other departing faculty.

As my family went off for our summer vacation a few days later, the idea of reusable bags was sticking in places I wouldn't expect or know until later. For example, the Katona family. Joey Katona was in my junior class at Harvard-Westlake that spring. I had taught his sister, Lindsay, a couple of years before. At the Katona family dinner table, Joey announced that Dr. Foster was leaving Harvard-Westlake to sell grocery bags. Apparently, this led to a lively family conversation since the idea that I would start a business was very strange behavior for a dyed-in-the-wool English teacher who had a Ph.D., after all. The whole family ended up, as a group, perusing my website later that night.

Joey's oldest sister, Karly Katona, was just out of college and working as a junior staffer for Los Angeles County Supervisor Yvonne Burke, responsible, among other things, for generating ideas for legislation. Karly liked the facts and figures on my website and thought this would be a good avenue for policy. Unbeknownst to me, throughout the summer and fall of 2006, Karly would build a case for this issue. Around county offices, she raised awareness of the ecological and financial costs of both paper and plastic carry-out bags. Over the next few years, this issue would become increasingly prominent in Los Angeles County and culminate in the LA Bag Ban in 2010, which became a landmark piece of legislation replicated in cities throughout California and across the US.

By the time I quit my teaching job in spring of 2006, I had placed four orders of bags from Amy, three with my logo and one for Cronig's. Even then, there was a lot to keep track of—where my inventory was, where it needed to go, who to pay and when, who owed me what. Already I had acquired a lot of expertise, not to mention inventory.

I discovered pretty quickly that becoming an expert was not only about asking the right question but asking the right person. For example, about that time, I was applying for a women-in-business grant from the Eileen Fisher Foundation. The application required a one-year estimate of revenue and expenses. I didn't know what a reasonable assumption was any more. My order rate kept surpassing what I would have deemed unreasonable just a few months before. Out to dinner with some friends, I laid out my problem as we ate. Right there, my friend's husband, a very sharp business lawyer, took out a pen, asked a few questions, and executed a business plan on a paper napkin. I was impressed and thankful. I copied his estimates into my application and became a finalist for the grant, winning $2500 to help defray costs that crucial first year in business.

So, when I needed to figure out how to handle the Cronig's order, I turned to Tony, my freight forwarder. I needed to get it on pallets and transferred to a truck. Tony introduced me to a third-party warehouse not far from the port.

When I asked Tony what a third-party warehouse was, he explained: They work with people who don't have their own warehouse. They take in freight and put it on a pallet, and store or load it onto a truck for you. You pay per carton.

This was another amazing service I had not dreamt of. I had been having bad dreams about forklifts, warehouses, and hard hats for some time. The idea that someone wanted to be in the warehouse business wiped away the nightmare.

Jim, one of the brothers who owned and ran the warehouse that Tony recommended, became my contact. He was a straightforward guy, laconic, but perfectly dependable and he ran a tight warehouse. In the years we worked together, we never once had a disagreement. He did exactly what he said he would do, and I did the same. I added new rows to my costing spreadsheet, but there was no way I could do this work myself. Now I had to find a truck to take the load to Martha's Vineyard.

I don't remember the trucker I contracted with for that first load. All I know is that high season on Martha's Vineyard traditionally starts on July Fourth. I promised Steve Bernier that I would get him bags before the holiday weekend. I was tracking the freight as it moved across the US. It was expected in Boston about the middle of the week before the three-day weekend. I thought that was plenty of time to get it to Cronig's, but the carrier let me know it would not be delivered till after the Fourth. I begged and pleaded, tried to cajole him, explained how important it was, but it didn't matter. The freight would not be delivered till the following week.

I'm not sure how I pulled off this stunt, but on the Thursday before the holiday, I drove into the freight yard in Boston in my station wagon. Looking up at the warehouse, I saw a bunch of guys looking down at me from the freight deck, not even trying to disguise their disbelief at seeing this small woman in a station wagon asking for her freight. It was more than a little awkward, but I stuck to my story. I wanted as much of my freight as possible to fit in the station wagon. I had discussed this with my freight rep, and he said that if I showed up, they would release the freight to me and charge me loading fees. Standing there, I realized that they didn't think I would show up.

They pointed me around the building to the office entrance, where I introduced myself and found my rep. He processed the paperwork and walked me out to the loading deck. He was impressed that I had shown up but couldn't understand why. I was not deterred. I'd seen that look before. The freight rep explained the situation to the men and pointed to my station wagon. One poor guy was picked to load up the car while the others had a good time ribbing him about his excellent abilities to load a station wagon and what an auspicious talent that was for his future wife. Loaded up, I thanked them and headed back to the Vineyard.

I pulled up at Cronig's just before 8 p.m. It was dark and I went inside to find the purchasing manager. She too had a look of disbelief, but she waved a couple of guys over to take the cartons out of my car and hike them into the back of the store. I was determined to keep my promises, and that turned out to be a good trait in a vendor.

Because I'd promised Steve at Cronig's that I would get him bags by the Fourth of July, because I'd also promised I would promote the bags in the paper, and because the Vineyard population is very concerned and protective about anything having to do with oceans, I talked my way into a front-page interview in *The Vineyard Gazette* where I was able to tell the tragic facts about plastic bags and the amazing new 99 cent solution for this problem to the entire Island on opening weekend.

*I was determined to keep my promises, and that turned out to be a good trait in a vendor.*

This was part of my tipping-point strategy. I treated everyone and everything in our favorite vacation spot like a super-connector and went out of my way to make facts, information, and bags available. This turned out to be far more successful than I could have imagined. The *Gazette* article came out, and when I called Steve Bernier to ask how it was going, he placed another order of bags right away and asked how fast I could get them there. I told him I couldn't promise I'd get them delivered before Labor Day, but I would do my best. Some things were out of my control, and I didn't want to make a promise I couldn't keep.

For the next two years, this is how orders would happen. I

would spend a few months securing an order, then wait a few months for production and shipping. Upon delivery, the store manager would reorder immediately and urgently. Sometimes within a day. Sometimes with an order twice the original size. I was in the beginning of a hockey-stick curve.

Super-connectors were emerging from unexpected places. I'd started the semester selling bags on the back staircase and ended with Tom Hudnut and Karly Katona promoting my bags to Ralph's and LA County. Expo West had thoroughly transformed me from high-school English teacher to eco-entrepreneur. Now away from Los Angeles and entrenched in my summer life, I saw super-connectors everywhere. Both my product and my message were resonating in unexpected places and brought me new friends and business partners who helped me connect to ever wider circles of people interested in and supportive of reusable bags. By the end of summer, I would be used to getting calls and orders from anyone anytime anywhere.

Some of these calls would result in long-term relationships. I received a call from Patricia Flint, who worked in advancement for Northeastern University in Boston. She had read the article in the *Gazette* and owned a house on Martha's Vineyard. The university's Marine Science Center was rebranding, and she thought my reusable bags would make a great swag bag for events. I told Patty that, as it happened, my daughter Daryn was the happiest freshman at Northeastern. We were so delighted that I wanted to donate 3000 bags. I'd recently negotiated a lower minimum order quantity with Amy, down from 8000 bags, which increased my sales to smaller stores who wanted their own logo on the bag. Patty was delighted. This was the beginning of a long relationship with the university that would eventually lead to my joining their Corporation Board, but that would be much later.

Also from the *Gazette* article, I received a call from Simon, then owner of Tags Ace Hardware in Cambridge, Massachusetts, and Vineyard summer resident. Simon bought 10,000 bags for his stores. When they were delivered in the fall, he immediately reordered a double quantity and promised to put me in touch with the import team at Ace Hardware. By the time I met them, I would have to fight harder than ever before to win that contract. Once I did, Ace was a fantastic and loyal customer over the next decade and one of my biggest accounts.

More mysterious was an unknown super-connector. I don't think I'll ever know who it was, but I'm sure it was someone on the Vineyard. Due to that person's efforts, sometime in the summer of 2006, I received an email from a woman in Philadelphia. She had received a bag or two from a friend who summered on the Vineyard, and she wanted ten bags to send to all of her friends. I sent her ten bags and included an invoice in the box asking her to send me a check, which she promptly did.

Not long after, I received an email from someone in Chicago who had received a bag from her friend in Philadelphia. She too wanted ten bags to send to all of her friends. I sent her a box of bags and an invoice, which she promptly paid. This pattern would continue throughout the fall and into the next spring. I came to expect a random email from a consumer—Kalamazoo, Minneapolis, St Petersburg (Florida), St Louis, and elsewhere—requesting ten bags. I learned a lot in those months about the power of trusting your customer and the power of networks. Even other people's networks.

Eventually, I received a call from a woman from the *St. Petersburg Times* in Florida asking for an interview. I don't remember how she'd heard of 1 Bag at a Time, but she was the best kind of journalist—chatty, easy to talk to, insatiably curious, and able to distill a message from a long and rambling discussion. The headline was: This Woman Wants to Change the Way You Shop. As far as I was concerned, she hit my message perfectly. I cut out the whole article, framed it, and put it up on my office wall where it remained for a decade, reminding me why I showed up at work each day.

My sister, after following what was happening, encouraged me to reach out to her local natural food store chain in Denver. I called the store closest to my sister, and the manager seemed interested. I sent her a sales kit and sample bag. After a few follow-up phone calls, she admitted that she loved the bag but didn't have the authority to make the decision. That was for the corporate office. Did I want their phone number? I did and cold-called Vitamin Cottage. They wanted a sales kit.

After a few email exchanges, they handed me off to one of their corporate product experts. He had a lifetime of experience in grocery sales. He was patient with me and gave me time to answer his questions. No matter what he threw my way, I jumped through every hoop. Finally, in the early fall, he wanted to know what colors were available, so Amy sent me a little stack of fabric samples. I cut out little squares and stapled them onto some cardstock, naming each color carefully.

In late summer 2006, my contact at Vitamin Cottage sent me their desired artwork in four-color printing. At the time, only screen printing was possible, and Amy was balking at even two colors. I realized that I needed to be able to handle artwork and invested in Adobe Illustrator 2, which came in a boxed set of CDs, took nearly an hour to load onto my computer, and cost upward of $3000. But I knew how important logos were to buyers and made it a priority.

I remember first exploring Adobe Illustrator on the plane back from the Vineyard in August. I spent the entire six-hour flight doing tutorials and figuring out how vector art works. I got lost in it. The tutorial explained how to draw circles of different sizes, then merge them together and erase the bottom half, so that it looked like a fluffy cloud. Then I made a sun by stacking concentric circles, making some of them zig-zag outward in various spikes. I merged those too and discovered a gradient so that the center glowed yellow and the edges orange. I created a blue sky that grew paler as it rose toward the top. Sometime toward the end of the flight, the guy behind me tapped on my shoulder and asked me what program it was. I turned to see a young dad with a little girl aged about 4 or 5 on his lap transfixed by the sunny scene I was drawing. I told him it was Adobe Illustrator and that it was amazing, but I warned him about the price.

By the time I was back in Los Angeles in the fall of 2006, I was coming to grips with the fact that I couldn't keep selling 10 or 20 bags to random consumers. I needed to get serious about an e-commerce site and hiring. Gary was getting more insistent about me getting an office. I had resisted before, afraid of getting ahead of my skis.

Then my cell phone rang. It was a buyer from Ralph's.

# Chapter 8

# Handling a Hockey-Stick Curve

How my sales packet traveled from the desk of Tom Hudnut to Robert Beyer to who-knows-where to land on the desk of Seth, in charge of grocery bags for Ralph's stores in Southern California, I will never know. Nor will I ever know what they told Seth. I think he was a little skeptical of the whole idea. In that first phone call, he just wanted to set up a meeting to discuss an order of bags with me.

I will never forget that meeting. I prepared for a week and a half, called friends for advice, created swatch cards, sales sheets, marketing ideas, and everything else I could think of. I was still unprepared. I assumed that I was pitching him, and that my goal was to convince him to buy the bags. That wasn't the case at all. By the end of the meeting, it was clear that he had a mandate to buy bags, and his goal was to find out if I could deliver an order big enough for Ralph's.

Seth is very good at his job. Later he would be very friendly and encouraging to me. I would work hard to earn his respect by performing in ways that surprised even me. In that first meeting, though, it was clear that he did not think much of my product, or me for that matter. He barely looked at the product and swatches I brought, and set about seeing if I could deliver what he needed.

Did I have corporate insurance?

Not yet but I'm happy to get it right away, I said.

Was I a corporation or a Limited Liability Company (LLC)?

I was neither, I was a sole proprietor, but I lied and said I was in the process of incorporating, which I was by the next morning.

What was the biggest order I could deliver, when, and what

was the price?

Up until then, I hadn't taken an order larger than 10,000. A couple of weeks before, Amy had told me that I had 35,000 bags on order, enough to fill my first 20-foot (6-meter) container, the smallest container size available. Amy advised me that I would save a lot of money if I filled containers myself rather than sending a few thousand bags at a time to the port and paying someone else to consolidate them in a container with other people's freight.

Actually, said Amy, it is much better to fill a container. Containers come to the factory, and we load everything ourselves. It is much safer, nothing can get lost.

My education in international shipping began. I learned that there were several sizes of containers. I didn't care much how many feet long a container was, but I started to care a lot about how many bags fit into a container. Amy told me the quantities of bags for each of the three most common sizes of container: 35,000 bags, 72,000 bags, and 84,000 bags respectively.

Biggest size container is best, said Amy. Much cheaper that way.

While I wasn't a numbers whiz, I committed those numbers to memory and, right now, in Seth's office, that was paying off.

When he asked me about the biggest order I could deliver, I offered him an order of 84,000 bags. It was the biggest number I could think of. He wanted 100,000 bags and asked for the price. I didn't flinch but I didn't have an answer. I needed a spreadsheet to work it out. I asked if I could get back to him the next day. We agreed to talk the next morning, and the meeting was over.

Although Compton, where Ralph's headquarters are located, is on the 405 Freeway and a straight shot north for me to go home in west LA, I ended up in the wrong lane and found myself on the 72 Freeway going east. I would have to go through downtown to get home. If you don't live in Los Angeles, it might not sound awful, but it added nearly two hours to my drive and was a complete traffic disaster. I didn't care. I wasn't just thrilled, I was out of my mind with excitement. I called Gary on the way home.

All the steps toward becoming a real company—steps that I had resisted—now needed to happen, and fast. I needed to incorporate. I needed liability insurance (Seth sent me the requirements, millions of dollars of coverage, numbers that I was not yet used to seeing). I needed to hire someone for boxing and shipping small orders because I was getting large orders as fast as I could handle them. I needed to accept credit cards. I needed a bank account for the business. I needed to get QuickBooks to manage purchase orders, customer and vendor information, invoicing, accounts payable, and accounts receivable. Spreadsheets were no longer working. I needed an e-commerce site so that smaller orders could come through over the internet and I wouldn't have to answer my phone at all hours and fill out order sheets.

I spent most of the ride home talking very rapidly to Gary about what I needed to do. Amazingly, he just listened and kept reminding me to keep my eyes on the road. My eyes were on the road, but my mind was somewhere else. It's a miracle that I got home safely, and very late after my detour through downtown. We ordered pizza that night. I was in no shape to cook.

With exponential growth comes an insanely steep learning curve. Within a few weeks, 1 Bag at a Time became 1 Bag at a Time, Inc. I had a bank account, insurance, accounting software, and accepted major credit cards. I remember being concerned by credit card fees. As my fees over the next few years skyrocketed, amounting to the cost of another employee, I would learn that there was an actual law that prohibited me from passing those fees on to my customers. It was another injustice that hit my moral compass, and I would find ways around it later. For now, I was ready to take a large order from anyone.

At the same time as I was working to get the Ralph's order, the buyer from Vitamin Cottage indicated he would order 100,000 bags as well. I was working with both of them to get their artwork right. Both ordered custom color fabrics, which Amy said was no problem. Custom fabric had a minimum order quantity of just 50,000 bags, which suddenly seemed like a modest number.

Getting set up as a vendor at Ralph's and Vitamin Cottage was more time-consuming and challenging than I expected, sending proof of incorporation and insurance coverage, filling out stacks of paper, agreeing to return policies, defective policies, and lengthy contracts and terms. I read every single contract, line by line, the way I read the Australian bag report, the same way I read *Anna Karenina*. I was trained not just to read texts closely, but to interpret them and commit them to memory. This came in handy. Again, I found my training as an English major to be exactly what I needed at that moment to understand the promises I was making. I took notes and made cheat sheets for everything I needed to remember.

I realized that I was accountable for toxicity and found a company that would test bags to prove my product was safe. I knew from the Australian report that the bag I was producing used materials with low toxicity, but I also knew that cheap manufacturers could add lead or other heavy metals to cut costs. I let Amy know we would test a sample bag for every large order, and she would have to factor in a few days for sample sourcing and testing to comply.

Where I encountered terms that I didn't know, I wasn't afraid to ask. Luckily, I didn't have to damage my credibility with Seth or other buyers by asking rookie questions. Both Ralph's and Vitamin Cottage had vendor specialists, patient and helpful people who walked me through the process as I checked off one requirement after another.

Sometime in early November of 2006, in exactly the same

week, Ralph's and Vitamin Cottage both placed orders for 100,000 bags each. I was working with Amy on pricing, scheduling, and getting sample bags that I could forward to the buyers for approval. When I received purchase orders from Ralph's and Vitamin Cottage, I turned around and sent my purchase orders to Amy. She was ecstatic.

Wa, Lisa! You are a big bag buyer now! she said.

As I had come to know, China was set up for big orders, the bigger the better. They are brilliant manufacturers and arrange their factories to churn out huge numbers of the same widget, day after day. Even small changes throw them off and there is pushback.

When an exporter like Amy goes to the factory with a big order, or two of them, they get what the Chinese call *face*. Roughly translated, that's respect. Her fortunes were tied to mine and to those of another big buyer she had, the one who had set her up in business a few years before, John. Suddenly, I had face too, at least I did in Changzhou, China.

At the time, I didn't have time to look back, but if I did, here's what I would have noticed. I had received my first order of 8000 bags a year before in November 2005, which took me five months to sell through. Now, at the end of 2006, my orders totaled over 250,000 bags, an increase of more than 300 times the year before. In 2007, I would sell 2 million bags, an increase of almost ten times the previous year, and in 2008 I would sell over 8 million bags, an increase of four times.

This curve is what every entrepreneur dreams about, but when it happens, it feels more like a nightmare. Problems that didn't exist before are suddenly very real and urgent. Foremost among them is how to finance that kind of growth.

As I placed the purchase orders from Ralph's and Vitamin Cottage, I realized their purchasing costs added up to more than my annual teacher's salary the year before. A lot more. I still had to pay for customs, warehousing, and trucking, and then wait 30 days for the invoices to be paid, while still more orders were coming in. Putting these orders into my spreadsheet, I estimated the cost of a full truckload and calculated how many trucks I would need. I priced them competitively, though I was still pretty sure I'd make a profit. Profit wasn't the problem. It was cash flow.

Six months earlier, I couldn't have told you what cash flow was. Now, looking at my numbers, cash flow was obvious and urgent. It was one of those weeks when starting my own business felt like an emergency MBA. Getting a lot of cash very quickly was going to be harder than incorporating or opening a bank account. A lot of money would need to go out in early January, and I couldn't expect payment till sometime in April.

I was lucky to have two choices to finance this kind of growth. Because I had purchase orders guaranteeing payment, I could have gone to the bank to get a business loan. I didn't want to pay interest, but as I look back, working with the bank would have forced me to have more financial discipline in my business dealings. It would have been a perfectly good solution and probably would have fueled my growth as an entrepreneur.

The other choice was to ask Gary to invest our savings in my business. Gary didn't balk when I asked for $6000 to start selling bags. Now I was asking for nearly 20 times that. This was not something to be taken lightly.

I was afraid of the talk I would have to have with Gary, but I have to admit, deep down, I was even more afraid of going to the bank. What if they didn't believe in me? I was still learning to believe in myself. I had a couple of sleepless nights trying to figure out what to do, and finally got up enough courage to show Gary the purchase orders from Ralph's and Vitamin Cottage, as well as the purchase orders I had sent to Amy to cover them.

I needed enough cash to pay Amy. He noticed the bottom lines of my invoices added up to a good deal more than I was asking to pay for the goods. There were other costs, I said vaguely. The cost of international shipping was still mysterious to me. I told him it was complicated but assured him I had crunched the numbers and was making a profit.

Gary has always believed in me. Overperforming takes a lot of work and, better than anyone else, he knew my work ethic. I offered to try to get a loan from the bank. He asked for a few days to think it over. In the end, he bankrolled me. I could pay us back in a few months when the purchase orders were paid, I told him. Of course, in a few months, my orders would double again, and I would have to reinvest all the profit I made to cover my next orders. It would be a while before I caught up to my cash flow needs, but within a year or two, I would have repaid us three times over the amount of the investment I was now asking for. If he had his doubts, he kept them to himself.

I continued placing orders for bags with my logo on them, which I resold at smaller quantities for higher profit margins, and now I was regularly getting orders ranging anywhere from 3000 to 10,000. By January 2007, I was on Purchase Order 26. My website, even if it wasn't the slickest website out there, was sincere and doing its job. My phone rang daily.

In early 2007, I hired my first employee. Sho was a recent college graduate, very committed to the environment, with a lot of energy, willingness to work hard, and no experience. His first job was to handle bags. I was still selling anything from ten to a hundred bags out of my dining room. Every day, when Sho came to my house, I handed him packing lists and labels. I was still generating labels manually by cutting and pasting information into the FedEx website, but it was still manageable. A few months later, I would spend a day or two on the phone with FedEx getting a dedicated label printer and syncing it up with my QuickBooks, which streamlined the process immensely. With a few clicks, I got a label. Another click or two and I had a packing list. It was a process that would come in handy later.

Then I started training Sho to take sales calls.

By this time, I had developed an order form, which I printed stacks of at a time. Having a physical sheet of paper for each order helped me remember who was in the process of ordering what and where they were in that process. Also, for me, it was still faster to write by hand than to type. The form reminded me of all the information I needed to make good on the promise of delivering a load of bags. I took most orders by phone, and sometimes it took a few days or weeks to get the art, colors, quantities, and other information nailed down. The logo was key, I knew, so the majority of my sales time was spent getting logos right and approved. When I had spare time, I checked my stack of incomplete order forms and emailed customers to remind them I needed an approval or a final decision about art or quantities. It was really helpful to have a paper trail to keep track of things.

I helped Sho develop good phone skills so he could answer the phone when I was processing orders and returning emails. He was a little sloppy at first, but I gave him a talk.

I said: Look, in school, if you get eighty-five percent right, you get a B and that's respectable. But in business it's different. How would you like to get eighty-five percent of what a business promised you? The standards are higher. When you make a mistake, it's going to cost me money and we need to run a tight ship here.

He understood and soon he was making fewer mistakes. Listening in on his conversations with customers, however, I realized I had another problem. Sho grew up speaking Japanese at home. Even though he was born in the US, he spoke as if English were his second language. I tried to explain how that sounded to a customer, how customers don't want to work with people they think don't understand them. Every grammatical mistake was a signal to the customer that he wasn't up to the task.

I asked him how it worked in Japanese, if he got a word wrong or made a grammar mistake at home. He said speaking poor Japanese wasn't acceptable, the Japanese were precise people.

Good, I told him, be precise in English.

To his credit, Sho took our conversation to heart, and he became an excellent salesperson, charming, a good listener, precise and exacting about confirming details and getting things right. Sho would work for me for the next seven years.

I learned how to manage customer expectations, giving them a realistic idea of when their order was arriving. Managing expectations was about keeping my promises. I started telling people that the lead time was three to four months, which didn't please anyone but seemed tolerable.

As things heated up in January 2007, Amy notified me that the lunar new year was coming and that in February, there would be no manufacturing for a month or maybe longer. I have to admit, I freaked out a little when she told me that any orders taken at the end of January wouldn't go into production till sometime in March and wouldn't ship till April. I realized that I would have to contact a lot of customers, explain, and manage expectations all over again. Delivery would happen sometime in late May, a lead time of five months for some, and as I would find out, up to six months for others. Amy and I would work more closely on lead times after that.

How factories could shut down for more than a month was a mystery to me. I came to realize that it wasn't just the factories. Business, government, schools—everything in China came to a halt. For the government, the break was just two weeks. But factory workers went home, which for most workers meant days on trains and buses back to the countryside they had left to seek a better life in the city and where much of their families remained.

Looking it up online, I saw that Chinese New Year is a massive, annual human migration, like nothing else in the world. Most employment contracts are canceled as everyone leaves for the holiday. When workers return a month or so later, they are free to look for new work. They come back to factories where pay is good and bosses treat them fairly. If they didn't like their last job, they take their chances on the next factory, hoping for better pay and treatment. Over the next few years, I would adapt to the rhythm of the Chinese calendar. The more I understood, the better I could make promises I could keep to my customers.

After incorporating my organization and figuring out cash flow, my next big project was an e-commerce site. Large orders were coming in regularly, and I realized that it took me the same amount of time to sell a box of ten or a hundred bags as it did an order of a few thousand bags, but thousands of bags were much more profitable. I made a few pennies per bag, so the key to profitability was volume. Still, you never know where a bag will end up, and I believed small orders would eventually drive bigger orders. I kept my website updated with answers to the questions I heard most often from people ordering fewer than a thousand bags. I thought if I could streamline those, Sho could box and ship them, and I would be free to work on larger accounts.

The internet was still in its early stages and e-commerce sites were new. Every site was custom built from the ground up. Homestead, which hosted my homemade drag-and-drop informational site, launched new design services for selling online, so I reached out. I wanted a site that looked like my informational site, only an e-commerce version with items to choose from, colors, quantities, and a checkout procedure.

I had a hard time convincing the site designer that I wanted it to look like my existing site. I'm sure the site looked terrible to her. For me, it was a brand image issue. People needed the information on my site to make the decision to buy, and I wanted their transition to the e-commerce site to be as seamless as possible. She said it was different technology and I needed a different URL for it, but I didn't want a different URL. She eventually worked around that with a subdomain. It was set to launch in early spring 2007.

In December 2006, I got a call from Laurie David. *House & Garden* magazine was doing a feature about going green and had asked her for suggestions. She told them about my bags. The only thing I didn't have at the ready for this opportunity was a promotional photo. I imagined a picture of one of my bags standing tall with carrot tops, a baguette, and maybe flowers peeking over the top. I'm not a great photographer but I decided to dig in and do it myself. It was a trial-and-error experience. If the carrots stood upright, a corner would buckle. If the bag stood straight, the baguette would tumble out. I found the sunniest corner of my house and brought standing lights from anywhere I could find them. Without a tripod, I used another stool to stabilize the camera. Later I would invest in good photography lights and a tripod, but this was my first attempt, so it was a little home grown. It took two or three days, but finally I got a shot I thought was good enough. I sent it to the editor at *House & Garden* along with a paragraph touting the benefits of going reusable and a link to my website.

Between training Sho, handling orders, getting my e-commerce site up and running, and dealing with logistics and the disruption of Chinese New Year, I had my hands full in the first months of 2007. I also found a small office that I could rent near my house. Literally, the ad on Craigslist read: Are you ready to move out of your home office? Yes, I was! It was an old complex of two-bedroom apartments from the 1940s or 1950s that the owner wanted to sell to a large developer, right on Little Santa Monica about a mile from my house. The deal was month to month, so there was no long-term lease, which was perfect for me. It was a little dingy, but I was so happy to have an office space that I didn't care. I spent a weekend getting a couple of Ikea desks and tables set up there, and the next week, I worked with Sho to move all the boxes of bags, tape, and label printers out of the house.

Gary and my girls were relieved to have the house back and hopeful we could finally host Thanksgiving again. I was happy to have a separate office where I could go for work and leave in the evening. I thought it would help me get some work/life balance, but that wouldn't be for a few years more. I still brought my laptop home every night to continue processing orders and work with Amy, but thankfully, there was no more boxing and shipping from the house. I negotiated with Amy to make sure the two large orders for Ralph's and Vitamin Cottage were shipped before Chinese New Year, so they were set to land in LA around the end of February for delivery in the first weeks of March.

After I sent the ETA to Seth at Ralph's, we had a number of conversations about display and promotions. I recalled my experience in Australia and encouraged him to think about two factors. First, I pushed hard to get him to display bags at the checkout stand where consumers were likely to need them most. That is some of the most valuable real estate in a grocery store, and most of it is sold to vendors willing to pay a premium. Because the Ralph's logo was on the bag, it was a branding opportunity for Ralph's, and he was able to justify using the counter to display them.

We also discussed changing the question at the checkout stand to: Would you like a bag? Flat out, Seth said that would not work. I tried another tactic. The cashier is often the only store employee a customer comes in contact with. How could you get cashiers engaged in alerting customers to this new product? After a few days, Seth had a brilliant solution. He offered a $50 Ralph's gift card to the cashier in each region who sold the most bags that week. He would run that promotion for his cashiers for a couple of months, depending on how it went. It would be a huge success. Cashiers were incentivized to promote the bags, and that's exactly what they did.

As if I wasn't busy enough in the first weeks of 2007, I also bought a bargain booth at Expo West in the basement and badges for me and Sho. We needed carpeting, samples, a table and branded tablecloth, a background image. The show that year is honestly a blur for me now, but I remember often having a line of people waiting to talk to me. I rented a scanner so I could scan the badge of everyone I spoke to for a record of who took samples. I would grow my email marketing list significantly. I met wonderful buyers that year who became established customers, many small natural food stores from Maine to Minnesota, California to North Carolina.

One day at the show, a group of people approached me. The woman in the lead said: I've been looking all over for you. It was Susan from Sprouts Farmer's Market. Sprouts was a small chain with big plans. Susan was an experienced buyer, and her career would rise with Sprouts' success. From this meeting, I would become friendly with Susan, and Sprouts would become one of my biggest accounts, taking a full container load every month for the next few years.

I booked rooms at a hotel a few miles away for me and Sho. As a trade show assistant, Sho was fantastic. He talked to everyone and knew his facts. Once or twice, he handled Japanese-speaking customers beautifully. He didn't tire easily and would willingly go back to the car in the parking lot for more sample bags when we needed them.

What I remember most from Expo West that year was talking nonstop from the moment the doors opened to the moment they closed. By 6 p.m. I didn't want to say another word, but I took Sho out to dinner every night and found the energy to show him how grateful I was. I encouraged him to order what he wanted and treated both of us to premium wines as a reward for good work. It was a long three days and worth it. We left with a lengthy list of new customers to follow up with the next week.

From March 2007, as orders grew, I focused on learning and

keeping up with the growth. I don't have a lot of memories from that time, but one day stands out from all the rest. Two things happened: my new e-commerce site launched, and *House & Garden* magazine hit the stands.

I thought I had timed everything perfectly and was pretty pleased. Our feature was a full page, option number 14 out of 20 Stylish Ways to Live Green. In my photo, the bag looked a little rumpled but good enough, and there was a write-up with my website and some statistics that now look a little outdated. It was online too, with a link directly to my site. Throughout the day, people started hitting my new e-commerce site and ordering. I thought everything was ready until the end of the day when I started processing orders.

*As seen in*

# HOUSE &GARDEN

FEBRUARY 2007

## 20 Stylish Ways to Live Green

### 14 >1 Bag at a Time

Lisa Foster discovered the concept of reusable grocery bags while living in Australia, where plastic bags make up about 2 percent of all litter. Last year alone she sold 75,000 bags to grocery stores made from recyclable polypropylene, the same material yogurt containers are made from. Each tote should keep 416 plastic bags out of landfills. www.1BagataTime.com

That's when everything ground to a halt. It turned out that the Homestead site had no ability to indicate the color of the bag desired on the packing slip or invoice. Actually, it was incapable of printing a packing list or a shipping label, only an invoice. As orders started piling up, I think about 300 small orders on that first day, I had no way to fill them. I called Homestead. After hours with tech support, sometime about one in the morning, they finally admitted they did not have the capacity to indicate the color of the item on an invoice and no way to turn the invoice into a packing list. Labels or a FedEx interface was not an option. They offered to refund my money.

At that moment, I didn't care about the money. I was frustrated, exhausted, and angry when they gave up. I would have to go online, look manually into every order, cut and paste the details into QuickBooks, and print packing slips and labels that way. That was on top of the other sales I took all day. I needed a website that worked.

Unable to sleep as the wee hours dragged on, I started browsing the internet to find a website designer, not as readily available as they are now. Somehow, I ended up on the Sprinkles Cupcake site. I'm sure I was hungry and looking for comfort food when I had no sleep in sight. Sprinkles made a huge splash that year by opening up a bakery that only made cupcakes. They were the most amazing cupcakes you can imagine, fluffy with fantastic flavors like red velvet, chocolate marshmallow, and bright strawberry. Browsing their website, I started wishing my website could be like that. Then I thought, Sprinkles had one item, cupcakes. I had one item, reusable grocery bags. They had flavors, I had colors. Whoever did their website could do mine. Somewhere on their site in tiny type, like that little tag inside The Essential Ingredient bag that had led me to Amy, I found a line: Designed by Ciplex.

That's how I met Ilya Posin, the founder and creative talent behind Ciplex, a website company based in Los Angeles. He was my first call the next morning. I don't think I was very coherent. Basically, I told him I want to be like Sprinkles.

You can't be like Sprinkles, said Ilya. But you can be a lot better than this.

I explained the kind of packing list I needed, and he understood. We made a deal to start immediately. The design lead, Zach, was great. We spent a lot of time discussing how to integrate all the information that I needed, the part of my company that was dedicated to helping consumers and stores learn the tragic facts about single-use plastic bags and the many amazing benefits of going reusable. In the end, we still needed two sites, one with the information and another twin site that was just for e-commerce. Each site had a link to the other in the top navigation menu. Though technically it was two sites, for the consumer, it felt like one seamless site.

Ilya and Zach together conceived of the site opening with a slideshow showing images of discarded plastic bags in the environment—an iridescent blue bag backlit and suspended in the ocean, a ragged one dangling from a beautiful tree, a twisted bag beside a family of ducks looking at it quizzically. The images were beautiful and haunting at the same time and imparted a tragic feel. The five facts about bags from my tag appeared as the slideshow rotated through.

Ilya sent me to a stock music site, which I didn't know existed—small bits of music you could purchase the rights to just as you could buy a freelance image on a stock photo site. I spent a long day listening to snippets of music and finally found one, a bit sad but in a lovely, elegiac way, and ending with a bit of an uplift at the end. It fit perfectly. A tragic tune with a heroic ending.

We ended the slideshow with a promotional image of my bags. I don't remember the message on that last image, but it was something like, You can save the world, 1 Bag at a Time. There were buttons to learn more or buy now. Ilya, Zach, and I spent a long afternoon going through the slideshow frame by frame, perfecting the timing so that captions emerged a fraction of a second after the image so the first impact was visual. Everything was timed to hit the right notes with the music. It wasn't Sprinkles, but it was a great site for 1 Bag at a Time, and I had it for years. Ciplex helped with a new, more professional-looking tag, with the same facts and a photo of a bag. As a result of the better site and SEO (search engine optimization), which they helped me with as well, 1 Bag at a Time became the number-one search result on Google for the next four or five years, a competitive advantage that was incalculable.

Somehow through all of that, I made it to April of 2007. I managed to deliver bags to Ralph's and Vitamin Cottage in time for the start of the month. Earth Day was becoming a month-long event, so timing was perfect. The first day the bags launched, both organizations sent me purchase orders for twice as much, 200,000 each, and the buyers were calling me asking when I could deliver. I said I'd get back to them the next day.

Amy needed to figure out how to ramp up quickly. We negotiated partial shipments for both large clients to arrive quickly, with the rest to follow as soon as possible. Sprouts was working with me for a container load that I would place by the end of the month, and they would place an order every single month for years.

Along with the rest, I ordered 20,000 bags with the 1 Bag at a Time logo to resell out of my little office. We would need to work with Jim at the warehouse to hold some of them as we could hold no more than 3000 bags at the office, but it helped us manage the flow of incoming orders. The hockey-stick curve inflected up again.

In the nature of all things converging when a tipping point is reached, Los Angeles County Board of Supervisors passed their first piece of bag legislation on April 10, 2007, officially asking the Department of Public Waste to conduct a study of bag impacts in Los Angeles County and recommend options for action. Passing that bill was a testament to Karly Katona, who had pursued this issue relentlessly, starting from that first night gathering facts on my website in the spring of 2006 after her brother Joey announced that his English teacher was leaving teaching to sell grocery bags. The study would lay the foundation for Southern California bag legislation over the next decade.

When the motion to commission the study passed, Karly listed me as a stakeholder and connected me to people in the Department of Sanitation. I had a few meetings with them and sent them copies of the Australian report, which helped guide their efforts. Because a lot of the science had been done, the

Australian report allowed them to focus on local impacts. Their report would estimate that in Los Angeles County alone, 6 billion bags were discarded annually. Although each one was a fraction of an ounce, together they amounted to 45,000 tons of solid waste a year, some in landfill and others requiring cleanup. Another 117,000 tons of paper bags were disposed of annually.[23] Early in the process, my contact there, Coby, said they realized that reusable bags were better in every single metric. The question for them was: how could they get a city of 10 million people to change their habits?

They began with stakeholder meetings and listened to what constituents thought. So, in April and May of 2007, I spent a few afternoons in the basement of a government building with other stakeholders, including PTA members who represented consumers, and people from environmental groups like Heal the Bay. I remember the representative of the PTA complaining about losing access to free bags and being clear that she and her friends certainly didn't want to pay for bags. I piped up with my knowledge of the hidden costs, helping them see that they were paying for bags but not directly, paying through higher prices for milk and light bulbs, and up to 17 cents per bag in higher taxes for cleanup, as found by San Francisco, amounting to millions of dollars for taxpayers.

By the end of the meetings, everyone agreed: the people of Los Angeles should know what carry-out bags were costing us collectively for cleanup and landfill of billions of bags. The report would later put that figure at $18 million dollars annually.[24] No one wanted higher taxes for what we started calling, billions of so-called free bags.

Coby told me later that they were surprised in stakeholder meetings to find grocery stores quite willing to promote reusable bags. Environmental groups such as Heal the Bay were already publicizing the impacts of plastic bags with images of entangled dolphins and sea turtles that tugged at heartstrings. As their efforts gained notice, consumers grew increasingly aware of the damage plastic bags caused, and grocery stores wanted to be aligned with their customers. The plastic industry was alone but well-funded in advocating for single-use bags. In the fall of 2007, after introducing legislation, Yvonne Burke invited me to be interviewed on her local TV show, and I spent an hour on camera debating a very polished plastic bag industry representative. I knew my facts and figures and never backed down, answering his objections with fact after fact. Again, my education in English literature proved helpful. If I had defended a dissertation in front of a panel of professors, I could take on a plastic industry rep.

No matter what the plastic industry tried, Coby and his team took the high road and dealt with them in good faith. When the plastic industry said bags were not the problem, littering was the problem, the county invited the plastic industry to mount an anti-littering campaign. When they did not, the county itself organized an anti-litter educational campaign, but the results were minimal.

Then the plastic industry demanded an Environmental Impact Report, or EIR, a costly and time-consuming review of legislative impacts, which they had a right to demand and which industries often deploy as a delay tactic or attempt to obstruct proposed laws. So, the county commissioned an EIR that included a breakdown of impacts for all 88 cities within the county borders. Later, when cities inside the county proposed their own bans, it pre-empted the plastic industry from using the EIR to obstruct legislation at the city level.

As Los Angeles County developed their bag ban policy, they were mindful of those for whom every penny counts and put in allowances for people on government assistance programs to receive reusable bags for free. They also worked to help existing plastic bag manufacturers develop reusable bag products and gave them low-cost government loans for equipment, so US-made manufacturing would increase.

These first legislative efforts culminated in the Los Angeles County Bag Ban in 2010, three years after the bag ban had been enacted in San Francisco. Soon afterwards, Calabasas and Long Beach adopted the ordinance largely unchanged from the county ordinance. The City of Los Angeles wanted to put their own stamp on their ban, but when they were challenged to produce an EIR, they revised their ordinance to match the county's. Cities followed like dominos after that. The LA County Bag Ban became a comprehensive model for cities nationwide.

Coby, who was then at the beginning of his career in public service, told me that everything he learned developing bag policy has been useful throughout his career. Karly indicated the same. As I look back, I see that, however hard and long the journey was, the effort to reduce dependence on plastic bags became a model of success not only for me, but for a lot of other people too.

As orders increased, I told Gary that instead of repaying the money we had invested in those first orders, I would need the profit I made to pay for new orders. I showed him my QuickBooks. I was making money on every order, but every penny was going out again to pay for the next container of bags. I told him I didn't know where this growth curve would end and that my cash flow was still tight, but I had no trouble with profit. As always, he told me to keep going.

# Chapter 9

# Key Account Management

As I was beginning to see, my real strength was selling. When a new customer called, I still got excited. All the skills I had learned in the classroom informed the way I went about my business. Students got excited when they understood, say, *The Great Gatsby* or *Macbeth*, how love and ambition drove people to extraordinary acts. I used the same tactics in selling, tapping into people's desire to feel heroic—the simple steps required to order. With every call, I felt I was truly saving the world, 1 Bag at a Time. It was on my website and on every tag. Every single day, I got up and lived that mission.

Having cut my teeth on Ralph's and Vitamin Cottage, I was ready to bite into other major accounts. Throughout 2007, I would add new key accounts, including Ace Hardware and True Value Hardware, and participate in my first reverse auction for a quarter of a million bags. Tony, my freight forwarder, and Jim at the warehouse became my good friends and key members of the logistics team that helped me move millions of bags into stores and consumers' hands that year. When things went wrong or I had a question, they were always helpful.

Others were patient and encouraging as well. Susan from Sprouts Farmer's Markets was a big supporter. When I met her at Expo West in 2007, Sprouts was embarking on a plan that would entail mergers and acquisitions and end in an IPO (initial public offering or stock launch) in 2013, positioning itself as a natural whole foods retailer with low prices. After the show, Susan sent me the Sprouts logo. I had already discovered that if people gave me bad art, and I returned a mockup with a good and faithful rendition of their logo, I would get the order. I never forgot what my first big customer, Steve Bernier of Cronig's, told me: If it's a grocery bag, it has our name on it.

I was teaching myself how to use Adobe Illustrator. The Sprouts logo was very complex—lots of colors, a cornucopia of fruit. I told Susan it would be more affordable if she could accept a one-color logo and she agreed. She asked for mockups in several color fabrics. I spent several days going through each piece of fruit—strawberry, watermelon, lemons—mocking them up on different colors. Later I would learn shortcuts, but at this time, I only knew how to change every watermelon seed and strawberry seed by hand. Whenever Susan asked for an adjustment or another color, I said, sure, and went to work. I never let her see how long it was taking me to get her what she wanted, and the work paid off. Eventually, she decided on a green bag and white logo. After that, Sprouts would order containers regularly for years and become one of my best customers.

Ralph's and Vitamin Cottage began to calculate their sales flow and sent me purchase orders regularly. Sho took care of any order under 3000, ferrying bags back and forth to the screen printer, and I was focused on selling orders direct from the factory to customers across the US. I was no longer surprised when someone called me up and wanted 10,000 or 20,000 bags or more, numbers that were impossible for me to imagine not long before.

Even in the heady days of 2007, I thought about how I wanted to position my company. I knew that I was among the first to market with this bag, along with Chico Bag and another direct competitor whom I would meet later, Stan at Earthwise Bags. Still, first-to-market is only an advantage for so long. As I looked ahead, I decided I didn't want to be the biggest bag vendor in the US. Holding that kind of market share would be cutthroat. I could sell a lot of bags, get a lot of *face*, or respect and buying power in China, but ultimately the margins would have to be razor thin. It seemed like a lot of work for not a lot of payoff. Besides, I didn't want to be forced into unsavory sourcing practices to maintain that position.

Instead, I decided to be the best bag maker. If you're going to try to be something, try to be the best. It was my motto. As other companies sold thinner fabric, and Amy offered cheaper prices for me to do the same, I resisted. Repeatedly, I would tell Amy, Quality is number one! We made quality control a cornerstone of our supply chain.

After a couple of misprints early on, we developed strict quality controls for imprinting too, with a photo of each new order emailed to me and forwarded to the customer for written approval before running production. We averted more than a few disasters that way. Our quality control and high-quality materials were a big part of being able to maintain low prices and profitability as we scaled up.

When I saw Jeffrey Hollender of Seventh Generation at Expo West in 2008, he was enormously pleased with my progress and asked me about the challenges I was facing. I told him that I'd been thinking about how to ensure my factories were not exploiting people. It didn't make any sense to solve one problem and contribute to another. When I broached the subject with Amy, she said, Oh, we only use good factories. No children, no, no, no.

I trusted Amy, but I felt I needed to do more than trust on this issue. Since the beginning of our relationship, I talked often with Amy about our need to align interests for mutual benefit. Apparently, I was not an average American buyer, there to push down prices at any cost. Even later as we bid on bigger contracts, she was always surprised during our price negotiations that I was concerned about leaving enough money in China to pay herself and everyone along the supply chain properly. She told me over Skype that she knew some companies were sourcing bags out of prisons and using forced labor. Neither of us wanted that. I was very clear: anything that was bad for her or for the factory workers was bad for me. We needed to work together, keep quality number one, and treat everyone with respect. These were core values for me from the beginning.

Jeffrey suggested that I contact Verité, a nonprofit started by his friend Dan Viedeman, who was dedicated to protecting workers' rights around the world. I called and was connected to Mary Jo Viedeman, Dan's wife. Mary Jo is smart and dedicated, a great partner, and someone who helped me understand even more about how factories in China worked. She explained that there were more workers than jobs at that time, so factory owners had a lot of power.

Verité's process was thorough and expensive. They not only talked to management but also inspected accounting and books. They interviewed workers on site and off site where they were more likely to divulge abuses. According to Mary Jo, as a communist country, China had labor laws that were very favorable to the workers. The problem was, there was little enforcement. Verité reports documented whether factories complied with local laws, and I was able to hold them accountable that way.

By 2008, I had the kind of leverage I needed. Mary Jo first asked me to write a code of conduct for the factories. She gave me a few examples that listed standards for forced labor, child labor, and other issues. I also wanted to include standards for environmental protection. I had already implemented toxicity testing for Ralph's and continued to test regularly for safe materials. Setting clear expectations for labor and environmental standards was one way I could use the power I was gaining in China to improve lives and ensure I wasn't unwittingly contributing to problems.

As I sat down to think about the standards that I wanted for my supply chain, I felt like I was writing a declaration of independence and wrote an eight-page document. Mary Jo suggested no more than two pages. *Right*, I thought. I cut it down, starting with a General Statement of Belief:

- We believe in respect for all people and for the environment.
- We believe in fairness, building trust through transparency, and solving problems in a spirit of openness, mutual understanding, and respect.

Then I set out clear expectations:

- No forced labor
- No child labor
- No harassment or abuse
- Fair and legal wages and hours
- Health and safety standards
- Environmental standards
- Compliance monitoring on demand

Mary Jo recommended that I include the statement about monitoring to make factories agree to unrestricted monitoring to allow Verité to do their job. 1 Bag at a Time was fueling a lot of growth for Amy and the factories she used. I let her know that if a factory wanted my business, they would have to agree to my code of conduct, allow inspections, and post a copy of the code of conduct in English and Mandarin where all workers could read it.

The majority of my bags were made by a factory owner whom I would come to know as Mr. Li. He was a good friend of Amy's, and sometime in 2007, he devoted his entire factory to making bags solely for me. He had about 90 workers, mostly women who operated sewing machines and a few men in the cutting room and screen printing. I ordered a Verité assessment and waited to see what I would find.

The ensuing report found some troubling issues, but nothing

horrible. The inspector found that workers were allowed to wear whatever they wanted to work, but because a scarf, belt or tie-string could get caught in a machine and lead to injury, they recommended that the factory order aprons for everyone to cover their clothes and tie in back for safety. They found some open ink cans in the screen-printing area and recommended that all chemicals be covered and labeled properly. They recommended that exit routes be clearly marked in tape on the floor.

The most troubling issue was payment. To motivate productivity, most cut-and-sew factories paid workers by the piece. Chinese law established minimum wages per hour. The more workers sewed, the more they earned, which made sense to align interests. To ensure quality, the cost of any bag that did not pass inspection was deducted from their pay. Sometimes, if a worker didn't produce error-free goods fast enough, their pay was below the minimum hourly wage. Also, there was no additional pay for overtime, which was required more often as my orders ramped up.

I asked Amy to work with the factory. The second Verité report, in late summer of 2007, found the easy items remediated, but the pay violations remained. I spent a long time on the phone separately with both Amy and Mary Jo, trying to see how we could deal with this issue. Amy defended the factory, saying their pay was standard for the industry. I pushed back, saying that they were not conforming to Chinese law.

After some time, I realized that the factory needed help in complying. I worked with Mary Jo, who finally divulged that Mr. Li's wife, who was the accountant, was keeping two sets of books and underpaying the workers. I asked Mary Jo to find out how we could help her learn to comply with local laws and pay workers properly. The result of these negotiations was a series of interventions by Verité that I would fund to teach the factory proper accounting standards. Like me, Mr. Li and his wife were entrepreneurs and made up a lot of business practices as they went along. If they were going to come up to standards, they would need help.

Throughout 2008, Verité implemented training at the factory at several levels, from floor safety to worker protection and, most of all, payment. To her credit, Mrs. Li began to keep one set of books and to pay her workers fairly. Amy worked with Mr. Li on measures that would help maintain prices and his own profitability while paying fair labor costs. As workers were treated better, they began to be more motivated, and productivity increased.

The world economy went into decline through 2008 and when it began to recover in 2009, China for the first time in decades hit a point at which there were fewer workers than jobs. Power shifted from factory owners to workers. Our orders were still rising through 2008 and 2009, and the factory was discovering that the workers all told their friends about being treated well and paid fairly. When other factories found it difficult to hire, this factory saw many workers return year after year, reducing their training costs and enabling them to ramp up production sooner after the Lunar New Year holiday. Although inspectors in China are generally regarded as a waste of time, Amy eventually thanked me for having invested in the factory. She told me once, You made our factory better.

By the spring of 2008, the factory had completed the remediation process and I ordered another Verité assessment, this time hoping for a clean report. When the report arrived, it showed that the safety and pay practices were indeed resolved. However, to my shock and dismay, there was a child labor violation. I was horrified and Skyped with Amy that night. What I heard from her was not at all what I expected and was more mystifying than anything else.

Yes, Amy told me, there is one worker a little bit young, but she is with her mother and sister, and she has her sister's face. For Amy, that explained everything, and that was the story she kept repeating. She has her sister's face. To me, it made no sense at all.

Over the next few days, between Amy and Mary Jo, who was in direct contact with the inspectors on the ground, I pieced together the story. Apparently in China, school was mandatory until 16 years of age, at which point students could graduate with the equivalent of a US high-school degree. However, the minimum age for working was 17. This created a gap year. More often than not, once they were out of school, young people had to get a job, and this was apparently a commonplace violation.

This particular family was a mother and two girls. They had come to the city just that year from the countryside. China lifted many millions of its people out of rural poverty by establishing capitalist conditions for factories to flourish in the cities and providing housing and jobs for those willing to migrate. I don't know for sure, but it is likely that this mother coming to the city with two young daughters, aged 16 and 17, was one of several wives of a rural landowner. It was common for wealthy rural men to have a first wife and a second wife, sometimes even a third wife. Because of the one-child rule, she would have been able to get legal papers for only one daughter, not the other. Regardless of whether she was a first or second wife, because she was unable to produce a male heir, she and her daughters were probably not treated well on the farm and lit out to seek jobs in the city as soon as the children were done with school.

What I do know for sure is that after Chinese New Year, when factories open their doors and begin hiring for the year, the three of them showed up looking for work. The factory was gearing up as quickly as possible and hired the whole family. When Amy said, She has her sister's face, she meant that the sisters looked alike and were sharing one set of papers. The mother was doing her best, taking care of two daughters, keeping them together, and helping them earn a living. They would not need to rely on the graces of a rural lord if they knew how to sew a straight seam, change a bobbin, and follow a pattern. It was one of those rule-breaking moments in China that was easy to look away from.

This left me with a dilemma. I needed a report that was free of child labor and other violations. Amy told me that the factory had offered to let the youngest member of this family go. It was unclear what the girl, or the mother and sister, would do then. Would the 16-year-old sit around at home alone all day, barred from work? Would she, or maybe all three of them, leave and try to find work at another factory with fewer scruples? At least at this factory, I knew they were treated well and paid fairly. The girl was six months away from being of legal age to work.

In the end, I told Amy not to fire the girl. That seemed too cruel both to her and her family, which was disadvantaged as it was. I found out when her birthday was and booked another monitoring report after she came of working age. I also told Amy to be very clear with the factory that in the future, anyone who applies for work who doesn't have legal working papers cannot be hired, and they made that promise to me. I monitored them over the years using Verité, and we never again had anyone underage or without working papers.

The whole experience was an eye opener for me and one of the hardest decisions I ever made. I would have to pay for yet another monitoring engagement that year. Still, I figured it was better for me to take that hit to do the right thing for this young woman, who had fewer resources and fewer options than I did, who was not herself at fault, and who didn't deserve to get fired under these circumstances. It seemed wrong to me that the girl herself, as a second child, was *ipso facto* illegal and could not get her own papers or exist legally. I hoped that allowing her to remain with her mother and sister at work was a kindness that would help.

Child labor violations had been a no-tolerance category of behavior for me, but the nuances of this incident demonstrated that the world didn't always work the way I thought it did. It was another moment when I realized that other countries existed on the other side of a looking glass that we might only be able to see through darkly.

My efforts to position 1 Bag at a Time as the best bag company, with marketing focused on two advantages—quality and ethics—paid off not much later when I got a call from Joe at Ace Hardware corporate headquarters. Simon, owner of the Ace stores in Cambridge, Massachusetts, made good on his promise to connect me. When Joe called, he was aware of the impacts of single-use plastic bags and generally in favor of reusable bags. Still, he had not sourced reusable bags for Ace Hardware. His hesitation was twofold, whether consumers wanted them and whether he could get the quality Ace wanted and the ethical standards he required in China.

Joe and I hit it off immediately. We had a long, rambling conversation about world problems—global warming, the accumulation of plastic, child labor, the pressure from big box and dollar discount stores to abuse labor to provide cheap, poor-quality goods here in the US. He was impressed with my efforts. Then he told me that as a hardware chain, they required high-quality products that would last, products that guys in hard hats could count on not to fail. If he was going to source a reusable bag, he said, it would have to reliably hold 2 gallons (9 liters) of paint from the store to the edge of the parking lot and back.

I told him of my monitoring efforts in China, told him the story of the girl with her sister's face, and was honest that I was waiting a few more weeks for her to turn 17 so that I could get the report I wanted. In my code of ethics, I stated that I valued trust through transparency. Letting Joe at Ace know where I was in terms of my efforts to ensure fair pay practices and child labor compliance built exactly the kind of trust I hoped to build.

He realized how deeply I was investing in ethical compliance in China, not an easy thing to do at the time. Joe saw that I had enough leverage to change working conditions and that I made the efforts needed to do it. As a merchandiser who specialized in international sourcing, Joe admired that. At the end of our conversation, he said, Well, now that we've solved the world's problems, how about you send me some sample bags?

I wish winning the Ace contract were that easy, but over the next few months, as it turned out, it wasn't. Earthwise and some other new entrants to the bag business were vying for this contract too. I would stay in touch with Joe through the bidding process. I kept my prices low. I got him mockups, sent toxicity reports, had my bags strength tested and reports sent. I found testing companies that would load 20 pounds (9 kg) of wooden blocks into the bag and put it on a machine with a robotic arm to lift and drop it any number of times. This too was a wonderful service to find. My bags showed no damage after 200 lifts and drops. Keeping the fabric thicker and ensuring good workmanship—my commitment to quality and ethics— was the right strategy.

I don't remember what else I did for the Ace bidding process. I remember being interviewed by several people on the import team. Most of all, I remember that for weeks, they would come up with some new test that I would have to pass. It was exhausting, but I hung in there. On a beautiful spring day, I received a call from Joe. I had won the contract, and he was calling to see what I needed on the PO (purchase order).

For a minute, I was stunned, but I recovered quickly. I thanked Joe and asked him why they had finally picked me.

First of all, he said, your bag was the only one that made it consistently to the edge of the parking lot and back with two gallons of paint. And second, well, you just wanted it so bad.

I didn't know what to say. He was right, I did want that contract badly. Besides being another one of those moments when I felt like my efforts were paying off, I knew that my passion for my product was the real secret sauce. That was something other companies would find hard to replicate.

In the years to come, I would work hard to continue to earn Ace's trust and business. I brought them new products, helped them with special products like convention bags and novelty products, kept them abreast of legislative issues

*My passion for my product was the real secret sauce.*

and updated on ethical monitoring, and called regularly to offer help for whatever they needed. I worked as hard to maintain this and other key accounts as I did to earn them.

After the Ace contract, I reached out to True Value. I let them know that I was supplying Ace Hardware and, before long, True Value ordered a container of bags from me too. It was a great example of how success begets success. No one wants to be left behind or miss out, certainly not retailers in competition with each other for consumer attention and market share. Someone from Aubuchon Hardware reached out and they became a client, too, soon after.

True Value threw some new requirements at me. They had a special security status for importing that gave them an advantage at the port. They submitted a lengthy form with 15 or more pages of highly detailed security requirements like perimeter fences at the factory and 24-hour lighting, as well as a schedule for inspecting the fence for breaches, and checking and replacing light bulbs. Amy and I spent a late evening, on my side, going over point by point security measures at the factory. Amy confirmed they had all these security measures, which were actually common steps used to keep burglars out.

At the end she asked, How do you know if really we have these fences and lights?

I took a moment to think, and I said, Amy, I trust you. If we don't have trust, we don't have anything. We might as well give up the whole business.

By this time, she no longer required me to send a third of my payment upfront when placing an order. My order rate was so fast that tracking deposits was an accounting nightmare. Purchase orders were routinely tens of thousands of dollars, sometimes in six figures. I remember the first time I sent her

*If we don't have trust, we don't have anything. We might as well give up the whole business.*

an amount that exceeded my annual teacher's salary in one wire transfer. A few months later, I would be sending her double that. My hands would still be shaking and my stomach aflutter hours later when I got home after a day like that.

That kind of trust takes months, even years, to build. From the start, we each expected the other to be true to her word. If anything was at the core of our success, it was that—our fidelity to each other and to our word. Neither of us ever violated that trust. If there was something we couldn't do, or if something went wrong, neither of us ever hid anything from the other.

Even though customers were reaching out to me, I had not stopped going after accounts I wanted. I was a lifelong member of Co-Opportunity in Santa Monica and loved their dedication to small farmers, quirky brands, and organic options. The Co-Op was an account I wanted, and I started calling. They were polite at first, and then strangely stopped taking my calls. I dropped by and asked for the manager a few times, who said the buyer was somewhere else and not available. Pretty soon, Co-Op began carrying bags from a competitor.

I remember chatting with Gary's aunt, another natural food aficionado, about my disappointment. Apparently, Gary's aunt knew everyone at Co-Opportunity. Unbeknownst to me, she went right into the buying offices and let the manager know he got that decision wrong. She demanded to know why they had purchased bags from someone who wasn't a member when they had a dedicated member of their own starting a grassroots movement to educate people about reusable bags and supply ethically sourced, high-quality reusable bags. Weren't ethics, quality, and membership what they were all about? Within a few months, the buyer at Co-Opportunity called and placed their first order. When I saw Gary's aunt at a family event later, I told her the Co-Op had called, and she admitted that she had gone in to advocate for me. It was another example of the power of networking. You just never know.

As I was in the throes of the hockey-stick curve, I opened my email one day to find an invitation to a reverse auction for a dollar store. I was getting used to big numbers, but I was pretty shocked to see that someone wanted a quarter of a million bags, and I was invited to bid. That was a lot of face in China, but I was a little wary. How would that affect the factory's ability to fill my other orders? I was getting repeat customers and understood that I needed to be a reliable vendor for all my customers if I wanted to build a business with staying power. I didn't want the factory tied up with one easy order for months.

When I talked to Amy, she said there were many factories that could help with large orders. No problem. You sell, we make. Easy.

I had no idea what a reverse auction was. I called the friend who had helped me find Tony, the freight forwarder, a year or two before. She said she didn't

*No problem. You sell, we make. Easy.*

know about auctions, but her boss would. She introduced me to Alan, who could not have been nicer or more generous. He explained that just as art or antique auctions helped establish the highest market price for a valuable item, reverse auctions helped mass-market stores establish the lowest market price for high-volume commodities. I would need to register and figure out how low I could go. When the auction day came, I could log on, and bid down the price until I either won or dropped out. Bidding was usually done in half-penny increments.

I created a sprawling spreadsheet for the reverse auction, trying to squeeze every last half-penny out of the supply chain. Amy gave me an excellent price and timeline. Tony said market forces drive shipping prices and he was subject to them. Getting a year-long contract for a shipping price would require me to be shipping things like refrigerators or cars, so I would have to rely on my own projections for international freight. I found a trucking company fully ready to work with me on consistent truckloads from one place to the other for a discounted price.

It was always surprising to me when people wanted business that repeated over and over again. I get bored easily and the idea of the same business operations for weeks on end held no appeal to me. I was glad others wanted that kind of work. Knowing my fixed costs, I calculated column after column of pricing, chipping away at my profit half-penny by half-penny, to the point where I would be losing money instead of making money.

When the day of the reverse auction came, I was ready. I printed my spreadsheet and taped it together in a long train so I wouldn't get lost scrolling on Excel. Alan agreed to be on the phone with me. Gary stayed home for the morning to see how it went too. My stomach was already churning as I waited to start. Then, bidding opened. I could see what I entered and the lowest bid.

I was pretty confident about my opening bid. I wasn't winning, but I wasn't far off, a couple of cents. I didn't know who my competitors were, but the low bid was always on display. I dutifully lowered my bid again and again as I watched the number fall. I was out of the bidding in the first ten minutes of the half-hour auction. For the rest of the time, I sat and watched.

If my stomach was churning before, it was wrenching now. After 30 minutes, I discovered the bidding extended another minute if a new winning bid was placed in the last 60 seconds. It was torture. Sure enough, the bid dropped in the last seconds and bidding was extended a few times before the price stuck for a minute without being challenged. When it was all over, the price, delivered to a warehouse in the southeast US, was lower than the best price Amy could offer me at the port of Shanghai. I wanted to vomit.

Alan said, This is how it works.

As I processed the experience over the next few days, I became very angry. Whoever had that low bid probably didn't have the buying clout to get a contract for below-market shipping—after all, it was grocery bags—so that factor was out of their control. They probably wouldn't get away with sneaking that many bags in without paying duty, so that was a hard cost too. I was getting a good deal on trucking, but I figured they could find maybe 10% cheaper trucking and warehouse fees than I was getting. Even with cheaper trucking and warehouse fees, their entire product cost was tied up in transportation logistics. They would have to buy the bags for almost nothing, engaging in unfair wage practices, maybe even forced labor—slave or prison labor. Fuming, I fired off a scathing letter to the CEO of the dollar business who, of course, never replied and probably never saw it.

As I would learn, there were a lot of mass-market businesses predicated on being the lowest price. Dollar stores and big discounters didn't want to know what their suppliers engaged in to win big in the US. Their customers complained about cheap Chinese goods while buying them by the handful. I was connecting the dots between the price we pay for goods here and the conditions of working people around the world. I would never again visit a dollar store.

A year or so later, I was at my sister's house for Thanksgiving weekend. Returning from the store, she held up a packet of three scissors in clamshell packaging and, in excitement, announced to everyone she bought them for five dollars! I didn't say anything. It wasn't her fault, but I lost my appetite for turkey that year thinking about the poor people who most likely made them. They were nice scissors, too.

After the reverse auction, I recommitted myself to the ethics and quality that I had established as my brand differentiators. I didn't need to make a killing, but if I couldn't make a decent living and ensure that everyone along my supply chain was treated fairly and with respect, I would bow out. There were things I would do, and things I would not do. If the entire US market for bags was a pie, I just wanted my slice. I wanted the slice of customers who cared about quality and ethics, who would pay a fair price and get a good product. It was grocery bags, after all. A few times in the years to come, I couldn't help chasing some large orders of a half-million bags or so, but I never had my heart in it and never won one. That was fine with me.

My orders would jump from 2 million in 2007 to 8 million in 2008. Amy and I acted as a team, smoothing out processes. As customers came back to reorder, I would be able to tell Amy what purchase order to repeat. Their screen-printing shop kept our screens around for a year, and because we didn't need to have customer approval on a duplicate order, repeat orders saved the factory a lot of time.

In early 2008, Adobe called me to produce a bag for their conference Adobe Max. I was thrilled to get an order from a company whose products I used and admired. The conference organizers wanted a zipper across the top of the bag. Could I do that? Sure, I said. Amy and I had developed insulated bags to keep groceries cold and we had a zipper on those. We could easily adapt that design and put a zipper across the top of our regular bags too. The order was for 8000 bags, which by then seemed a modest number.

That year I moved our offices from the apartment-like space to a real warehouse space nearby. There is a little industrial pocket near the freeway between Wilshire and Santa Monica boulevards. It wasn't the cheapest warehouse in LA by far, but I didn't want to be far from home yet and I could afford it. I still had one daughter at home and, with orders doubling every six months, I stayed late at the office often.

By this time, I had four people working for me. Besides Sho, there was Andrea, the receptionist and my assistant—dedicated, sharp, incredibly accurate and, to me, indispensable in keeping bills and invoicing straight and on time. Also, I had a couple of warehouse and logistics people, none of whom lasted very long but I was always grateful for their help. I took in my own freight now, and no longer needed to pay Jim for in-and-out fees. My orders began to catch up with cash flow, and I started to pay myself a salary. I kept my promise to Gary to double my teacher's salary in 2007 and far more than that in 2008, putting back into our accounts several times over the investment we made the year before.

Sometimes I would stare at the ceiling at night and consider how many people were now making a living from 1 Bag at a Time. Besides my little team, there were truckers and freight brokers who took freight every week to every corner of the US for me; Tony and his team helping us with international freight; and a few hundred people in China whose lives depended on my next sale. It was a lot of responsibility, and I was well aware that none of this was about me or 1 Bag at a Time. The fewer mistakes we made, the more efficient we got, the better it was for everyone. I focused on quality control and did my best to keep things moving.

In spite of my best efforts, sometimes things went wrong. That's what happened with the Adobe Max order. Somehow, at the factory, they had reversed one side of the zipper in a way that made it impossible to zip.

When we discovered the problem, the bags were already in my warehouse. It took me a couple of hours to get up the courage to call the client. Their convention was a few weeks away, and I needed to let her know I could not deliver on my promise. There was nothing I could do but apologize. She was furious and I didn't blame her. I knew she needed to vent and let her vent on me for a while. She finally hung up to search for replacement bags and I'm sure it cost her a bundle. While my repeat customer rate was well over 80%, she was not going to be one of them. If there was a problem, it was my responsibility. If things went well, it was because I had a great team putting in the effort to keep this engine running.

Amy offered to rebate me the cost of the bags, which was fair, and I accepted. Amy and I always took responsibility for our mistakes. It was up to Amy to go back to the factory to get them to take responsibility too, which they always did. It was an incentive to ensure accuracy and quality in the future, and also about expecting relationships of trust down the supply chain.

Even when we were selling millions of bags, we had an overall record for quality that was excellent. Ralph's, Ace Hardware, and True Value all used automated systems to track and charge us back for bags that customers returned. Out of 100,000 bags, we were getting average charge-backs for three or four bags. It was an enviable record.

As 2008 came to a close, I was finally catching my breath. I reached out to my biggest customers at the time and asked them why they stuck with me. I saved the email from Seth at Ralph's from December 2008. He wrote:

Lisa

You had a competitive bid, and you provide non-monetary value as well. You're also the current vendor of record with a spotless shipping record. All bags always scan properly. Your product is never involved in any complaints due to lead issues, etc. You maintain testing to ensure child labor laws are maintained. You attend to and fill us in on all issues regarding plastic bag/reusable bag legislation. I know there are others, but these are the ones I thought of off the top of my head.

Good luck.

I was doing a lot of things right. If I could keep my head down, keep my promises, ensure ethics and quality along the supply chain, communicate with and excite my customers, I might be able to make this into a real business.

# Chapter 10

# Know Your Vendors

I'd been doing business with Amy for almost four years before I made my first trip to China. We had become increasingly emmeshed as business partners. By 2009 I had a team in LA experienced enough that I could leave for a week to meet her in person and see for myself the factories I was doing business with.

Since I quit teaching, I'd worked 10- or 12-hour days six days a week or more—sometimes much more. Sales, as I knew well, drove the entire machine. If I stopped selling, the whole thing would collapse. Truth be told, I loved nearly all my customers and loved the interaction. I had become, through and through, the Bag Lady. So, whether I was in LA, on the Vineyard, or traveling, the sales pipeline continued to flow.

When we were planning the trip, Amy told me the name of a nice hotel in Changzhou, and I reserved a room. I booked a flight to Shanghai in the economy section, which was expensive then, over $2000. I wasn't concerned about the seat. At my height, sometimes my feet don't touch the ground even in coach.

I cleared customs in Shanghai and walked out bleary-eyed. From years of Skype calls, I knew what Amy looked like, but I didn't see her anywhere. We had built a relationship on trust. Now I felt foolish. I didn't even have her phone number programmed into my phone. The signs were all in Chinese. I felt like kicking myself. Maybe I trusted too much. I started looking through emails to find her phone number. Before I got it, Amy came running up to me with a dozen red roses in her hand.

Sorry, so sorry to be late, she said breathlessly. We went to the wrong door. Airport so big!

I was so relieved. She hugged me warmly and my fears subsided. She took my carry-on and suitcase. So heavy your shoulder-bag! she said.

I told her I needed my computer to send her more purchase orders tomorrow. We laughed. My sales pipeline flowed into hers. Amy booked tickets for us on the bullet train from the airport to Shanghai. She wanted to show me the city before we went to Changzhou and got to work. Excitedly, she pointed out that we were going over 400 kilometers an hour, well over 200 miles per hour. The scenery whizzed by. It all felt a little surreal, like a different magic kingdom.

I hadn't slept well on the plane and was feeling overwhelmed. I needed a couple of hours to nap, shower, and check email. By mid-afternoon, I felt more clear-headed and met her in the lobby. Amy escorted me outside to see the Bund, Shanghai's historic business district built in the 1800s by the British. Filled with stout, stolid buildings, it was lovely and familiar. Even the weather seemed British. The late March wind was pleasantly brisk, the sky cloudy but not rainy. We walked down the street to the waterfront, strolled a few blocks beside a pretty barrier wall with built-in niches for plants all over it. Hanging flowers and vines cascaded downwards, covering the entire wall. We peeked over it to see the harbor.

After some time exploring, Amy found a little neighborhood and said this would be a good place to eat dinner. She asked someone walking by for a restaurant recommendation, and we walked into a little café. It was a tiny place, not a dozen tables in all. Amy and I sat down by a window, face to face. It was the most amazing meal I've ever eaten. I have no idea what most of it was, but it was all delicious. Braised tofu with a salty sweet soy glaze. A plate of tiny whorled shells with very thin red and blue stripes swirling into the center, no bigger than a thimble, each like a work of art. Sucking a shell, I got a spoonful of warm, briny broth and a salty bite the size of a caper.

More amazing than the food was the connection Amy and I clearly felt for each other. We sat for over two hours, talking like best friends, which we were. The things that delighted one of us delighted the other. We talked about grocery bags far longer than anyone might imagine possible, details of imprints, shipping requirements, the many things that went wrong, our sometimes-fumbling attempts to make them right, laughing at our own foibles and excited about the clear overall success of our partnership. We spoke rapidly and finished each other's sentences. We giggled at half-spoken thoughts. I marveled in the middle of it how much we had in common, how alike we were in our desire to be good at our jobs, to keep our promises no matter what crazy stunts we pulled. Amy was the Chinese me. How lucky I felt to have found her! We would do anything for each other. Together we felt we could do anything.

The next afternoon, Amy's husband picked us up and drove us to Changzhou. We passed apartment complexes for what seemed like hours. Finally, apartments gave way to countryside—great rolling grasslands, sparsely populated with short, squat, red-roofed houses, situated beside well-watered fields.

The air in Shanghai was like the air in Los Angeles on a bad day. As we drove into the countryside, I was surprised to find that the air was no better. Smog seemed to hang over the whole country. It was a persistent reminder of the toll that fossil fuels were taking. Smog is a local problem, but emissions are a global issue. I hoped our efforts to help Americans reuse plastic would lead to reductions in global net emissions as reusable bags replaced trillions of single-use bags. The vastness of the problem reminded me that we were a tiny piece of a much larger puzzle.

In Changzhou, I was pleasantly surprised by the hotel's elegance. The lobby had polished marble floors, gleaming brass accents, and chandeliers in the lobby. The rooms were well-appointed. I told Amy we would start at ten the next morning. I fell into a routine that I would follow for the next six or seven years visiting Changzhou. I would rise around 5 a.m. and order a pot of coffee from room service. I was hard-pressed to convince them, day after day, that I wanted a whole pot of coffee, not just a cup. I'd do half a day's work from my hotel room, managing sales and email, then go up to the hotel gym for a half-hour. That gave me time for a quick shower and to be ready at ten for a day with Amy.

That first year, I was there to learn—who were the factory owners, what was important to them, how was the factory set up, what difficulties were they having, how could we improve communication and production times. In subsequent years, we would develop intricate fabric color-coding systems and develop new products. They could prototype overnight, and I could review them the next morning in Amy's office, a process that would take weeks and hundreds of dollars if we used FedEx.

Before I talk about Amy and the factories, I have to talk about John. John is Amy's mentor, her first and best customer, and probably her best friend. Here's how I met John. I was sitting in my office, the little converted apartment office space off Little Santa Monica, about a year before my first trip to China. The phone rang, and I heard a deep voice with a British accent say:

I've been watching you.

Before I could recover my wits, the voice went on. I'm a friend of Amy.

That was really enough to silence me. Amy is well known in her city, but who in the English-speaking world would know Amy?

As I would learn, John is a Brit who has spent his life sourcing and selling goods from far-flung countries, mostly China but also India, Japan, Taiwan, Vietnam, and elsewhere in Asia, into English-speaking countries like Australia, New Zealand, and Canada. He has sold everything from gym equipment to sneakers, but since the early 2000s when reusable bags swept across Australia, bags have been his primary business.

John likes to take credit for having discovered Amy. She was John's account manager when he first began sourcing bags.

She worked for an exporter who contracted with factories to manufacture goods. John, an old hand at selling, found himself with very large orders very quickly. He brought an order of a million bags to Amy's boss, who after several talks, would not commit to a price. Frustrated by the evasiveness, John was ready to find bags elsewhere. Amy, as the account representative, felt responsible and tried to help him negotiate a deal. Over dinner as she made her case, it occurred to John that Amy was talented and knew a lot of factories on her own. He suggested that she start her own business and that he would source bags from her. He said he would help her.

It took John some months to convince Amy to leave her job and start her own export company. Amy began to see the value in being her own boss. True to her character, she gave proper notice and left on good terms.

She quickly earned a reputation for being fair, quick with numbers, and detail oriented. John would place multi-container orders for a million bags or more which would be delivered over time. With orders like that, Amy had *face* at factories from the beginning, and she knew how to use that kind of power.

On that first phone call, John told me that Amy had started out exporting bags from a factory owned jointly by Mr. Shi and Mr. Li. John gave me a brief history of the two men, and I found John to be an excellent storyteller. The story he told was this.

Mr. Shi worked for the government until a few years ago and did very well. He has excellent connections and is good in business, but he doesn't know anything about making bags. Mr. Li has no experience in business, but he knows how to make bags. He manages a factory floor very well and turns out a very consistent product. He's known to cut corners every time he can, so he needs a good eye on him to hold his feet to the fire. Amy does that very well.

This was the same Mr. Li running the factory when Verité inspected for labor violations, so John didn't need to say more.

It was good to know a bit about Mr. Li's reputation, which matched what I was learning.

John went on with his story.

Mr. Shi and Mr. Li had had a falling out a few years back, and now, each was running his own factory. Amy tried to place about equal quantities of work with them and play to the strengths of each. Mr. Shi was interested in developing new products and learning new techniques. Mr. Li, on the other hand, wanted easy work. The bigger the order and the simpler the design, the happier he was.

It was enormously helpful to know Amy's background and that of my primary business partners. John already knew what I would come to learn, that knowing your vendors— their strengths and weaknesses, their personality, likes and dislikes—is a competitive advantage. I later realized that John was mentoring me, as he had done for Amy.

Amy, the daughter of an accountant, was educated as an accountant. She is intuitive with numbers and has a sharp mind for business. Even early in her career, she knew how to be assertive in ways that gained her respect and had a confidence that helped her stand out. Right out of university, she spent a couple of years modeling. Then she followed her father into bookkeeping, taking a junior position at the firm where her father worked. She was promoted early and often.

One day, walking down the hallway to a meeting, her father came up from behind her. Apparently, he didn't like the way she swished when she walked. Why do you walk like that? he demanded. Amy just laughed and kept on going.

Amy is slim and smiles easily. She is just as happy at a business banquet as she is at home eating with her family. Most nights, Amy's mother cooks for the family, who all live in the same building in an apartment complex made up of several identical high-rise buildings. To me, they were dizzying. How easy would it be to enter the wrong one and end up in someone else's living room? When I asked Amy if she ever mistook another building for her own, she laughed as if that would be impossible.

Every meal we ate, without exception, was a traditional Chinese meal with soup as the central dish and various side dishes. Rice is ubiquitous, but to my surprise, they eat little of it. It's used more as a filler in case you are still hungry after everything else. Nearly always, there is watermelon for dessert.

Once, at a banquet with the factory owners we worked with—the tag maker, the screen printer, a couple of cut-and-sew facility owners—I asked Amy what they ate for breakfast.

Same, same, she said, waving her chopsticks over the food.

I thought about what that would feel like—Chinese food for breakfast, lunch, and dinner for years on end, maybe 80 years or more.

In America, I said, breakfast, lunch and dinner are very different. Breakfast is usually cereal or eggs, lunch is a sandwich and maybe some soup or a salad, and for dinner usually meat and some vegetables.

I figured you have to talk about something, and it was best to avoid topics like politics or international trade. Food seemed a safe topic, or so I thought.

Amy translated what I was saying, and no one said a thing. So, I went on.

We have food from all over the world. If we eat Chinese food Monday night, then Tuesday we might have Italian food like pasta or pizza. Wednesday maybe Mexican food or Thai food. Sometimes, we just eat American food like hamburgers.

Amy translated and again, the entire table was silent but only for a moment. Suddenly they all erupted in laughter so loud that it startled me. It took me two days to figure out what they thought was so funny. They were thinking: *Why would you eat like that when Chinese food is obviously the best?* Talking about food, I had inadvertently stepped on their national pride. Luckily, they were amused.

Later at that banquet, they would start drinking in earnest and fall into a deep stupor, slurring their words and literally falling off their chairs. It's a wonder they didn't crash on the way home. Amy and I never drank at these dinners and would leave early, never wanting to be on the roads past about 8:30 p.m. A couple of years later we would have a banquet with the factory owners' wives too, and after it, Amy would tell me of a screen printer's terrible temper when he was drunk, how he abused his wife, how stoic she was. Sometime later, he lost his business in an alcoholic binge, letting the business founder. It's a pity, Amy said. Such a good screen printer.

Always first on our list of factories to visit was Mr. Li's. By the time I met him, Mr. Li had converted his whole factory to manufacturing my orders. Walking in, I was not just his biggest client, I was his only client. Amy drove me to the factory along dusty streets to a small parking lot and up an admittedly dingy staircase. Mr. Li rented two floors of a manufacturing space and outfitted his factory with sewing machines, cutting equipment, one-color screen-printing equipment, and an office.

The office and workshop spaces were much cleaner and more brightly lit than the corridor. I first met Mr. Li in the office, along with his tiny, demure wife. In all the trips I made, she never once sat at the table with us, but I noticed she was always in the room and attentive. I found Mr. Li to be as eager to please as he was to impress. As the recipient of my efforts with Verité, Mr. Li was quick to point out improvements that came from that engagement. When we walked through the factory, he gestured to a wall-sized poster of my code of conduct written in English and Mandarin, smiled at the bright blue aprons that everyone wore over their street clothes to ensure no frill or belt would end up caught in a machine, and pointed out clearly marked walkways and signs for the exit doors, and other basic safety measures. He spoke only Chinese, while Amy translated. He agreed with Amy that these changes were positive and helped improve safety and professionalism at the factory. I imagined what it might have looked like before it was cleaned up and was glad that I had invested in Verité. The people here had a clean, safe place to work and were paid fairly too.

I remember being amazed at the efficiency and speed of the Chinese factory. Every step in the production process is broken down to an action that can be completed in a few seconds, then repeated time and again by one person whose job is to just do one thing. In the sewing room, one group of mostly women sewed handles onto the front and back panels. Another group sewed on the side piece. Yet another made the final seam sequence to connect all the pieces. At the end, inspectors checked the finished product and, if it passed, sent it to a folding table. There, more women sat inserting countless bottom stiffeners, tagging, folding, and stacking the finished bags into groups of ten. Sometimes as we toured, a worker would pause and look up at us, smiling or curious, but that was rare. They were paid by the piece, and they could complete a piece in three to five seconds. Looking up was costly.

On the first floor, below the workshop, was the print shop. One-color imprints were handled by two men who imprinted a panel very rapidly, in less than two seconds. They moved like dance partners, transferring unprinted panels one by one from a huge stack onto the imprinting station, passing the screen and ink over it, and from there to a drying rack. Innumerable racks lined the walls with wet panels. It was exquisitely timed with no room for hesitation or variation. They were in the zone, men with machine-like rapidity and accuracy. It was amazing.

Equally dumbfounding to me was a small room designated for sewing handles. There were two heavy machines that needed little skill to operate, designed solely for this purpose. A young woman sat at each one, feeding into one side of the machine a 2-inch strip of fabric from an enormous spool at her feet. Out the other side came a neatly folded, precision-sewn handle with seams on both sides and the edges tucked inside. Seemingly miles of handles were piled in great hoops on the floor higher than the desk they worked at. When the spool was done, the worker set the empty spool aside and started in on another.

I tried to imagine guiding a strip of fabric through a machine for four hours, a break for lunch, then four more hours of the same. I imagined going home at night, eating dinner, falling asleep, and coming back the next morning to do it again. And again. For someone as easily bored as I am, that kind of monotony was impossible to fathom. It seemed to me a particular room in hell, a punishment beyond words. The girls there looked up briefly and smiled at us as we peered in, their machines clicking away. Conformity in China is a norm, unlike the US where we are an entire nation of non-conformists and individualists. We sell, they make. They are brilliant manufacturers.

Most of the factory workers I met in China — in all the dozens of factories that I visited — were happy and contented with this kind of repetitive work. I don't mean to imply there aren't unsavory factories, only that Amy didn't work with sweatshops or places that used forced labor. She worked only with well-run factories, which are plentiful in China.

Once, touring a factory where they had their own cafeteria, the lunch bell rang as we strolled through the workshop. To my astonishment, the still, focused faces all came alive. There was quite a hubbub as the workers discarded their aprons and emerged in fashions of all kinds. It was just like a high school breaking for lunch, with guys flirting with girls, girls giggling in groups, and all of them racing down the stairs to eat and socialize. Peeking in at their lunch some minutes later, we saw a few of them look up curiously to check us out, but most were happily engaged in conversation, laughter, and moving about.

Their work lives apparently didn't hamper their social lives. I was as relieved as I was surprised to see that happy change in them. I never would have guessed it from seeing them on the factory floor. Once, on my third or fourth trip, on our way out to lunch after the factory tour, I would witness an altercation. Mr. Li had parked his car in a way that blocked a truck in the parking lot. The driver accosted Mr. Li as we came out, and the decibel level spiked immediately. They stood inches from each other, yelling at a volume that is not heard in America, little bits of spit flying in each other's deeply red faces. I could feel the rage and indignation, the unwillingness of either side to give ground or lose. Eventually their rage subsided, without resolution. It was too intense an emotion to sustain for very long. Mr. Li and the driver both backed off without coming to blows, which surprised me. Apparently in China, yelling matches are acceptable, but there is little physical confrontation. As we got into the car and went to lunch, Mr. Li apologized. It took us all a while to shake it off.

Year after year, Mr. Li took us to a small local restaurant for lunch and ordered alligator soup. I wasn't sure it was legal, but even from the beginning, I knew his pride was at stake. In China, I would always do my best to enjoy what was served, which meant being a good sport about alligator soup for years. He always asked if I liked it, and I always said, yes. Validated, he would refill his bowl and happily engage in conversation.

Most of the time, no one would eat unless I ate first. I made a point of trying every dish and putting on a good face no matter what was put in front of me. Ceremoniously, everyone would watch as I tried one dish then another and approved. Once everyone was busy eating, I tried to stick with vegetables, often quite wonderful and delicate.

After lunch, we would visit other factories. For two- or three-color imprints, there was a separate screen-printing factory with tables that stretched 20 or 30 yards down the whole length of the workshop floor. They had rulers at the top of the tables, and blocks to guide a frame. Hundreds of fabric pieces were placed side by side down the long tables, then a guy with one framed screen went from one to the next, using the blocks to guide placement, squeezing one-color ink onto the fabric, taking maybe a second each. When the printer was done, the whole team went outside to have a cigarette while the ink dried. In China, ink is not cured by heat at all, not even very low heat. Printed items are left to dry with only ceiling fans. Once one color dries, the second screen with the second color is lined up precisely over the first color. It was hard for me to believe the accuracy of this work. Print after print was perfect, each swipe of ink taking a second or less. The imprint that day was an order for a small private school who would give them out at their annual fundraiser.

To see my orders in the process of production was thrilling. I sent a breathless email that night to my contact at the school, if email can be breathless. I was so excited that I broke protocol to send photos of her bags in production. She was equally excited. It was just a grocery bag, I know, but to her and to me, it was a statement about the environment, about their identity and community. It was just a bag, but it was a symbol of much more. And symbols, I knew, were powerful.

On every trip, Amy and I would save a day to drive about an hour and a half to meet Mr. Zhu, the fabric maker. Mr. Zhu, then in his mid-thirties, was taking over management of the factory from his father, who was retiring. Mr. Zhu was quite tall with a young son of his own whom I would occasionally glimpse riding around the factory on a tricycle. I met him first at lunch before touring the factory. Over the meal, he talked endlessly to Amy about an order for tons of fabric to go underneath couches at Ikea, barely acknowledging me.

That first visit, Mr. Zhu never once spoke directly to me. I would later admire their fabric-making machines, which came from Germany. They are enormous, two stories high occupying a space about half the size of a football field. He spoke to Amy about how they operated and then waited, looking away while Amy translated.

Back in his office were a few guys, his driver, and some others who formed his posse and were apparently on payroll. They would all smoke at once and I would have to ask Amy to open a window. Here I was clearly not an important customer and he made sure I knew it. Eventually the father came in and we all stood up, shook hands, and made pleasant talk. Amy had their respect, which was good, and she was very deferential and at her most pleasing with the father.

Amy was fiercely loyal to this company. In China, factories pop up and disappear overnight, and investment in machinery is rare. Between me and John, she understood that high-quality products drove the business, and good fabric was a central component of her strategy. As I watched Mr. Zhu over the years, I came to see that he was proud of his family, proud of his factory, and proud of his country, not just proud of himself. Most Chinese, I learned, like most Americans, wouldn't live anywhere else.

There was also a shy, demure, soft man, Mr. Huang, the tag maker. He was a good printer, very precise, had his own shop which he'd inherited from his father, who was a friend of Amy's father. It was as much a friendship group as a supply chain—personal connections like currency in an industry needing many parts.

Amy would say later, each person was an important part of her network. She saw them as her team and treated each member well, bringing their talents together to make a product she was proud of.

I once asked Amy if she was the largest bag supplier in China.

No, I am largest supplier here in Changzhou. There is another lady in Shenzhen. She makes many bags.

Around Shanghai, though, Amy was quite well known. When factory owners had a problem, they came to Amy. A few years later, Amy would tell me about one factory owner who gambled away his money to the point where he was too far in debt to make payroll. She lent him money, saved his business, and worked with his daughter to step up and take control of accounting and keep her father in line.

Only once in all the years I visited did I see Amy get angry. We were at her office between factory visits. Walking out, Amy asked me to wait a moment and stuck her head into a little side office where her long-time accounting associate, Chloe, did the books and generated official documents. Chloe spoke limited English and was reliable, accurate, and loyal to Amy. Seemingly out of nowhere, Amy began to yell at Chloe in very rapid, very loud Chinese. Chloe said something and Amy came back even stronger. I didn't know what Chloe had done, but at that moment, I was glad I wasn't Chloe.

After a few minutes, Amy turned to me and said, Let's go.

Walking down the hallway I was tense. Finally, I said, Are you going to fire Chloe?

Amy laughed all the way to the elevator. No, no, no, she said. You must yell at them. Otherwise, they think it is okay to make a mistake.

And that was that.

In the fall of 2009, Amy emailed me a few photos of bags in a style we were not making, more tote bag than grocery bag, with interesting colors and imprints. She said a man had come to her office from a few hours away, out of the countryside, where he was making a lot of them for the US market. The exporter was not treating him fairly and he heard Amy was fair, so he asked if she could be the exporter for this client. On one bag, I saw a big Old Navy logo printed on the side piece.

I reached out to Nancy Green, who was then Head of New

Business Development at The Gap, Old Navy's parent company, to see if she could connect me. Years ago, in one of those coincidences that make the world seem small, Nancy and I had been roommates at the University of California, Berkeley. I was the nerd with my nose in a book while Nancy was starting her career in retail, working at a boutique while taking classes. Later, she steadily worked her way up at The Gap. Nancy graciously connected me to the Old Navy buying office, and I went to meet them in their Bay Area offices that fall.

They were wonderful to work with and happy to have a new vendor for their tote bags. They explained their buying system and how they put together a season of new products, designing everything 9–12 months ahead of time, getting bids and vendors for every item, using color-matching systems to make sure that everything from sneakers, to T-shirts, to tote bags came together in a seasonally appropriate, color-coordinated whole. Designers, buyers, and logistics all worked together on tightly controlled deadlines to make sure a look would hit stores at exactly the right time.

Working with Old Navy was another stretch moment for me. They needed new designs every quarter. I sourced samples and created bids for each item, which when accepted went immediately into production.

I loved their artwork, filled with positive messaging and happy bright colors—peace, love, hope, pink, yellow, green. It was a steep learning curve, but the art made it fun. Old Navy spoke a world of acronyms—EDI, JFM, DPO, SKU, ASN, and on and on. I couldn't remember them, so I created a cheat sheet for me and my team. Repeatedly they stressed on-time delivery and the seriousness of delivering late.

The details were insane. I spent a lot of time managing my team. Everyone had a part, from getting colors and production details right on the production side, to logistics details on my side: tracking incoming product, sorting boxes by style and destination, printing shipping labels and making sure the right label got on the right box in the right place, and coordinating with truckers to pick up on time. In my warehouse, every carton in and every carton out got checked and double checked.

On the first order, after months of on-boarding and product development, everything was coming together on schedule. Until it didn't. A monsoon hit China particularly hard around Shanghai. Amy called me to say they would be a week late. The ink, it wasn't drying. There was flooding everywhere, people drowned in Shanghai, every house, every factory, was damp for days. We had to wait.

I was terrified to notify my buyer. How many times did they tell me about on-time deliveries? How would one late item affect rollout of a season? But there was nothing I could do. There were certain production realities that were beyond my control. Ink needs to dry.

I finally got up the courage to call my Old Navy buyer. She was upset, and I steeled myself for a chewing out. To my surprise, she checked the news stories regarding the monsoon, and calmed down quickly. It was bad, she agreed. There was nothing I could do about the weather. Explanations were made, schedules were adjusted, and I never shipped another order late again.

When you walk into a store like Old Navy, everything fits together as if it all came from one big factory, but I realized that every item, from the smallest socks to the wall of denim to the racks of T-shirts, were sourced from thousands of small vendors like me all over the world.

I would never walk into a large store again without sucking in my breath at the brilliant effort it took to pull off season after season. Amy and I were a tiny piece within these enormous economic forces. The energy of American creativity and business partnered with the manufacturing genius of China and factories the world over. Because it is powered by fossil fuels, this economy has its environmental costs. If we could switch to renewable energy sources and reduce and reuse plastic, it would be a sustainable system. Even as I write, people today are working on the infrastructure for just that switch.

Working with this retail giant, I began to see that we are all intimately connected. We were so alike and so different, just different sides of a looking glass. The millions of Americans purchasing foreign goods are a mirror image of the millions of Chinese who manufacture them, wanting the same things—to live in safe and healthy communities, to take pride in our countries, to have meaningful work and contribute to something larger than ourselves, to support our families, to raise and educate our children, to celebrate the important days with family and friends—birthdays, graduations, weddings, births. If you look past the borders, if you're willing to open your heart and mind to the people on the other side, it's a beautiful system that creates what each side wants. Amy said it best: You sell, we make.

In winter 2009, I walked into Old Navy in Los Angeles and saw my bags saying Peace on Earth amid the thousands of other items to buy. It's really hard to describe the feeling.

I know mine was such a small part in the wide world, but coming from teaching, starting a business to help Americans switch to reusable bags, and finding myself facing a wall of fashionable and inspirational reusable totes at Old Navy had been an unlikely journey. Who would have thought that young women across America might want a bag of their own with positive messages to take their stuff to work or school? What were the odds that a bag maker from the interior of China would come to Amy, activating a network of relationships from Amy to me, to Nancy, to the buying team at Old Navy, and now bags made by 1 Bag at a Time were hanging on the floor of Old Navy? It was some sort of full circle. My tipping-point strategy tipped. I had quit teaching to change the way America shopped, and if young women wanted these bags, I started to think that maybe I had done what I set out to do: changed the way America shopped.

## Chapter 11

# Become Efficient as the Curve Flattens

Sometime in 2009 when I was hair-on-fire busy, my daughter, majoring in business at Northeastern University, came home for some holiday and told me, You know, that's a thing. When your business goes up exponentially. We studied that in my business class.

Even though I was caught in a hockey-stick growth curve, I wasn't thinking about it as a curve. To be honest, I didn't have time to think about it.

Looking it up, I saw that no matter how high your curve goes, eventually it flattens. Considering what was likely to happen to my sales curve ahead was sobering. Competition would eat into my customer base. Eventually, trying to stay in business would be a long slow slog with low margins. That's the tragic life of a commodity trader.

Looking at the back side of a hockey-stick curve, I was glad that I was dedicated to quality and ethics from the beginning. I was not going to show up on the front page of a newspaper for exploitation of the environment or humanity, and neither were my customers. I dealt with companies that valued that commitment and that understood that a fair price was exactly that, a fair price. It brought me a lot of loyalty, but I knew there would be a limit even to that.

I would have to become more competitive to survive. Looking at my business expenses, I felt there were two places where I could sharpen my pencil. The first was credit card fees, which were costing me almost as much as another employee. At the time, it was illegal to pass those fees onto my consumers, so my options were limited. I had persuaded millions of shoppers to go reusable, so I put the same skills to work letting clients know that we accepted payment by credit card, but to remain competitive, we preferred to be paid by check. Within a year, I reduced my credit card fees by 90%.

The other area where I felt I could improve efficiency was in trucking. After shipping millions of bags across the US, I became familiar with the ways of truckers. Very early on, when I was still operating out of the little office in Santa Monica, I used C.H. Robinson to carry what was for me, at that stage, a large load, 6000 bags on two pallets, to a customer. To my surprise, I was charged twice.

I called them up and said, This is impossible. There were two pallets. You are charging me for four pallets.

The agent at the other end of the line said, I just go by the paperwork. I have two sets of papers signed, saying they were received.

No matter how hard I fought, C.H. Robinson insisted on being paid double for that load. Lesson learned.

I put in a system to communicate to my customers precisely what they were getting and that they were responsible for signing only for cartons they received in good condition. I developed a PDF drawing of what a pallet looked like. It

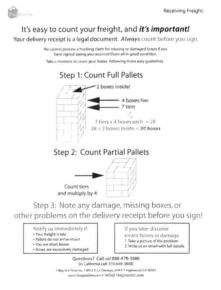

Receiving Freight.

It's easy to count your freight, and *it's important!*
Your delivery receipt is a legal document. *Always* count before you sign.

We cannot process a trucking claim for missing or damaged boxes if you have signed saying you received them all in good condition.
Take a moment to count your boxes following these easy guidelines.

Step 1: Count Full Pallets

— 2 boxes inside!
— 4 boxes/tier
— 7 tiers

7 tiers x 4 boxes each = 28
28 + 2 boxes inside = *30 boxes*

Step 2: Count Partial Pallets

Count tiers and multiply by 4

Step 3: Note any damage, missing boxes, or other problems on the delivery receipt before you sign!

| Notify us immediately if. | If you later discover errant boxes or damage. |
|---|---|
| • Your freight is late | 1. Take a picture of the problem |
| • Pallets do not arrive intact | 2. Write us an email with full details. |
| • You are short boxes | |
| • Boxes are excessively damaged | |

Questions? Call us! 888-478-3886
(in California call: 310-649-3888)

1 Bag at a Time, Inc. • 8915 S. La Cienega, Unit F • Inglewood CA 90301
www.1bagatatime.com • info@1bagatatime.com

illustrated how we got 3000 bags on a pallet and explained how to count freight quickly. Communicating was powerful, and I never had a signing error again.

I blackballed companies that tried to cheat me or that proved unreliable. Brokers from C.H. Robinson begged me for a decade to give them freight and I told every broker my story and explained I would not do business with a company like that, and I never did. By the end of 2009, my freight process worked pretty well, and I kept my expenses under control.

The most embarrassing trucking incident involved a load of bags that were a promotional item for a new condominium development, I think in Florida, to be used at their grand opening. Bags were ordered, arrived in my warehouse, and shipped on time. A week later, my contact called me, concerned. They hadn't shown up. I called the trucking company. They assured me the freight would be there the next day. But the next day came and went, and the next and the next.

The grand opening was a few days away, and my contact person was nearly in tears, thinking she would be fired. I called the trucking company and escalated the issue as high as I could go. They admitted they had lost the freight, there was a frantic search, and the day before the opening, the bags arrived.

My customer asked her staff to bring a few cartons up to the administrative office so she could show her boss and team. To her horror, the cartons were scribbled with lewd drawings, obviously the handiwork of a bored warehouse worker somewhere. She was mortified, and I felt her embarrassment. I sent photos to the freight company, who discounted the load for the mishap, and I passed the discount on to my client. It was not nearly enough to account for the damage done to my customer and my reputation. The freight carrier was blackballed.

Only once in all my years of shipping did I have a barcode error. Barcodes are really complicated, and errors are common. When I was first learning how they worked, Joe at Ace Hardware referred me to Chester, Ace's resident barcode expert. I didn't know there was such a thing, but apparently barcode specialists have their own conferences and spend days discussing the minutiae of barcode standards, symbology, and development.

Calling Chester was one of my favorite things to do. Instead of being a stickler or a bore, Chester was surprisingly and indefatigably chipper and wry, even when talking about barcodes. And he was always talking about barcodes.

One day, my phone rang, and it was Chester. This was odd— usually it was me calling Chester—but I was happy to take the call. In his pleasant, upbeat voice, he said, I have bad news. Your cartons have the wrong barcode on them.

Now, this was a reorder. Amy and I were good at this. I asked Chester if he was sure the carton marks were wrong. Chester, of course, was sure about the barcodes. All 840 of them, the whole container. I asked him to send me a photo.

I sent the photo to Amy with a note. She rang up the carton factory. It took several days for them to get to the truth of it. They hadn't used my artwork. Someone at the carton factory had generated new bars using the right numbers but the wrong symbology. In the end, the carton factory took responsibility, printed up 840 stickers with the right bars, and FedExed the stickers overnight to Chester directly at Ace. Amy gave me a credit for over $800 to repay the fine from Ace, and she collected from the carton company.

It's a great credit to Amy that she was able to leverage her status to get this factory so far down the supply chain to own up to their mistake and pay for it. The tendency at factories is to look away, deny wrongdoing or mistakes, leaving customers feeling burned and looking for a new vendor. It was a testament to how Amy built her supply chain on relationships and how she managed factory owners exceedingly well.

My business by this time was stabilizing. I consistently had one or two and sometimes three containers on the water headed toward the Port of LA. New customers were still calling me to order bags. I worked hard to please my customers and optimized the website as best as I could, so I didn't have to prospect for clients yet. At the dinner table, I felt I had good news to share often.

One night, I was talking about my day when Gary suddenly said, Stop.

I paused and looked at him.

He said, I don't want to talk about grocery bags.

It caught me short. Gary was always supportive, but I had to admit, the details of who ordered what was admittedly mundane dinner conversation, at least for someone not directly involved. True, he talked about movies nearly every night, but Hollywood is inherently more interesting than commodity orders. I made a mental note to not bring business home with me.

When I couldn't talk about bags at home, sometimes I found myself not talking at all. Often, I would opt to spend evening hours on Skype with Amy to whom I could talk about bags endlessly. It would take me a while to sort out what really was interesting about my business, not the details of orders but the people. Later I would come to Gary with people problems — Gary is brilliant about people, especially difficult people — and he was always engaged and helpful.

But my silence had a limit. Even if Gary didn't want to hear about the details, I still needed to manage them. Once in a while, I had to remind him that I couldn't always stop when he said stop. One year, on my birthday, Gary got us tickets to the symphony and a reservation at one of the best restaurants downtown. I was excited about going, but as evening rolled around, I had business to take care of. Shanghai is 14 hours ahead of Los Angeles. When Amy is getting to work at nine in the morning, it is five in the evening in Los Angeles.

That day, I needed to negotiate. I think it was shipping schedules, which became difficult around Chinese New Year. The negotiation was delicate, important, and detailed. I could hear Gary pacing and calling to me that we had to go. There was traffic and we had a dinner reservation. For a while, I didn't reply. Eventually, he came halfway up the stairs and insisted that we were going to miss dinner if I didn't leave that minute. The pressure from both sides suddenly got to me. I told Amy to wait a minute and went into the stairwell to lean over the banister. I'm negotiating with China, I yelled down in a voice louder than I intended. If we're late, we're late. I don't care if we have to eat peanuts. I'm working. Then I turned around and went back to deal with Amy.

He wasn't happy about it, but he stopped yelling at me. Things shifted after that and he never yelled at me again, no matter how late my business took me.

Around 2011, I moved my offices to a bigger warehouse space near the LA airport. It was farther from my house but perfect for me at the time, much nicer and more affordable than the warehouse I had rented closer to my house. Upstairs were two clean, carpeted offices, a meeting space, and a big window overlooking the warehouse floor down below. It had its own loading dock.

Soon after we moved in, I hired Shannon, who saved me more than once. Shannon is about 6 feet 6 inches, a former college basketball star, enormously reliable and fiercely loyal. He broke his office chair a couple of times a year just from sitting in it and was almost comically oversized for the upstairs Ikea chairs around our conference table for weekly staff meetings. He called me Boss and was always there when I needed him. The warehouse was his space and he protected it.

When he first came to interview for the job, sitting at that Ikea table, he took his wallet out of his back pocket and put it on the table to avoid having to sit on it. After we spoke for some time, I invited him downstairs to tour the warehouse. As we left, I noticed he left his wallet on the table. Was this a guy who felt comfortable and safe? Was he someone who was so big that he knew no one would mess with him? Either way, I immediately felt a sense of safety and trust, and I knew right then I'd hire him. Later, as things became difficult for me, he was a steady, calming presence in the office and the warehouse.

Not long after he came to work for me, I took two full container loads, one bound for Ace Hardware and another for Sprouts, into my own warehouse on the same day. Over 50 pallets in all. There were no in-and-out fees, no palletizing fees. We hired two temps to unload and palletize that day. There was hardly space to walk in the warehouse when we closed up that night, just a tiny tunnel like Peter Alexander's house with boxes of PJs or my dining room a few years earlier. But this was a warehouse, so the scale was different—over 160,000 bags all at once. From the window up above, I could see pallet after pallet. The next day, Shannon rolled the pallets off the loading dock onto two trucks in the most efficient warehouse process I could imagine. It was a beautiful thing to see. Shannon was king of that warehouse.

He was a good king too. I remember one night, working late when Shannon was getting a final load onto a truck. I popped in to see if we were ready to close up and overheard him listening to the truck driver's woes. Apparently, the truck driver had girlfriend problems. Shannon listened empathetically for a while, letting the guy pour his heart out. Afterwards, Shannon made him feel accepted, a man among men, and then Shannon told him how much he loved his wife and two girls, how his wife always made him a better man than he could have ever been alone, how her love was the one constant in his life and how he felt a deep gratitude for her acceptance. The truck driver listened. Shannon's voice was soothing.

We need them, don't we? the truck driver asked.

Yeah, Shannon said with his big easy laugh. That we do!

The driver locked and secured the truck door, Shannon pulled back the loading ramp and leaned it against the wall. I faded back and left without letting them know I'd seen the moment. It was too intimate, and I'd been an interloper. Shannon was a natural maker of men. I wished then that I could have done more for him and offered him more opportunities.

Efforts to regulate single-use grocery bags in California ramped up in 2010. San Francisco had passed a bag ban three years before and there was increasing pressure for Los Angeles to do the same. The patchwork of city regulations was becoming a problem for retailers like Ralph's or Ace. If a Ralph's in Santa Monica, under restrictions of a bag ban, stands across the street from, say, a Safeway in another jurisdiction where they can give out single-use plastic bags by the handful, they have a competitive problem.

About that time, I received a call from a local lobbyist, whom I'd met casually at a few events. He explained that Stan from Earthwise Bags (my most direct competitor) and Andy from Chico Bag had hired him to the tune of $10,000 each to represent the reusable bag industry in Sacramento and Washington, DC. I was a little surprised, but I didn't say anything. Then he said something to the effect that Stan and Andy had decided not to include me in their efforts, but he said confidentially, he thought I should have a chance, so if I wanted to, I could pay him $10,000 and he would bring me in.

I was a bit confused and told him I'd think about it. He made it sound like he was giving me a seat at the table, but as I thought about it, he was already contracted to do this work. I didn't see that my money would have any effect at all. Besides, I wondered, why hadn't Stan and Andy called me? Was it because I was a woman? We had collaborated on some efforts before, and I thought I had a pretty good relationship with them, but now, I wasn't so sure.

The more I thought about it, the less confused I was. By the next day, I had the good sense to be insulted. I called him back and let him know I wasn't interested. If they wanted me to contribute, they would have to invite me to the table properly.

A few months later, my contacts in the environmental

industry brought me to the table when the issue reached the state level. They were organizing a lobbying day and wanted me to participate. In August 2010, 50 or 60 people from city governments, consumer groups, and the reusable bag industry all flew up north for the day to meet with lawmakers. Stan and I were paired up to make our pitch for reusable bags. I was to start conversations with the tragic facts about plastic bags and the heroic qualities of the bags we offered; Stan would follow with the business case, talking about leveling the playing field, jobs, and savings to the state for cleanup.

Our first meeting was with Mark Murray, the Executive Director of Californians Against Waste. Decades ago, he had been successful at getting regulations passed for recycled paper in California, particularly for paper bags.

Mark was unkempt and had steely blue eyes that didn't blink much. It was unnatural and a little unnerving. He made it very clear from the outset that he was not interested in our facts and figures. He was singularly focused on recycling. He looked us both in the eyes without blinking and said, I'm going to regulate you out of existence.

There was nothing Stan and I could say, and that's how the meeting ended. I would meet people like Mark later, people who would kill you to save what they perceived was the environment. I noted it didn't engender much inspiration.

Stan and I together shook off our encounter with Mark. We had legislators to meet. By and large, our conversations went well. Legislators took samples, heard us out and promised to consider our point of view, and were mostly polite.

Mostly. At the end of the day, we stepped into the offices of Lois Wolk, and everything that was working for us turned wrong. When the senator joined us, she asked us to be brief. I had a distinct sense that she was hostile to us from the get-go. Admittedly, Stan and I were off our game. I'd been starting conversations, but this time, Stan jumped in first. I followed with more facts and figures, trying to see what would resonate with her. After a couple of minutes, we knew we'd lost her attention. She watched attentively as a group of men in suits walked in. She interrupted us and said: Sorry, but I have bigger fish to fry. With that, she got up and walked away. I was stunned to be treated like that from a lawmaker. After AB 1998 was defeated, it came out that the plastic industry had spent nearly $50,000 to defeat the bill, mostly through direct donations to individual senators, including Lois Wolk.[25] Rarely had I been treated so rudely. Bigger fish to fry.

My goal was always to inspire consumers. I have always trusted that people would make the right choice on their own, without politicians and lobbyists in the way. After that day, I would continue to speak out for reusable bags and write a few op-eds, but I never again got directly involved in legislative efforts. It was a dirty world and didn't fit my ethics. I felt that, in the end, most American consumers cared about our environment and would, by their own choice, increasingly turn to reusable bags regardless of legislation. And I was right. The numbers would prove it in the years to come.

In November of 2010, Los Angeles County passed a bag ban covering the 88 cities within its borders, largely to very high public approval. It would be another six years before the state of California would put the matter to voters directly as Proposition 67 to ban single-use bags statewide, a measure which passed despite the well-funded campaign to destroy it.

Bags are still available at checkout in California with a mandatory ten-cent fee for either paper or plastic, and there has been remarkably little backlash from consumers. The state and oceans have clearly benefited. Plastic bags dropped from 73.5% of all litter collected on coastal cleanup days in 2016 (then the number-three litter item collected behind cigarette butts and fast-food packaging) to 1.5% of the litter collected in 2018.[26] As I drive around Los Angeles now, I only occasionally see bags wafting over the roadways. Most people don't remember that bags used to hang everywhere in our cities and environment. It's hard to notice something that is no longer there, but that's okay. Better that the bags are gone. It wasn't about getting noticed.

Somewhat to my chagrin, I was getting noticed. Most notably, Northeastern University was noticing me. After I gave them 3000 bags for the Marine Science Center when my daughter Daryn entered as a freshman, I would occasionally get a call over the next couple of years when a professor was in Los Angeles.

I didn't think much of these visits until, one day in 2011, I received a call from my contact at Northeastern. Would I be available to meet the University President for lunch? She gave me dates when he was in LA. I told her that Gary would be away, and I expected they would decline. *Surely, he wanted to meet Gary*, I thought. But no, it seemed fine that Gary would not be there. Why did the President of the University want to meet me? In all honesty, I was a little intimidated, but there was no backing out now.

As we sat down, President Aoun immediately put me at ease. He was there with his Senior Vice President, Diane MacGillivray, and they both were so friendly that I forgot to be nervous.

It turned out that President Aoun was at the University of Southern California when I was getting my Ph.D. there, so we had friends in common. A linguistics professor by training, Aoun was lively, talking about the importance of language and communication, a topic of interest to us both. When Aoun asked me how I'd ended up selling reusable bags, I told him my story. At the end, he asked, How can we get you more involved in Northeastern? I told him maybe I could come speak to an entrepreneurship class. He said, Done, and so ended a perfectly delightful lunch.

Soon after, I was invited to speak to their business school in a more formal event than I was expecting. I was comfortable in a classroom, but I wasn't so sure about making a keynote speech. Public speaking still stumped me and left me gasping for air. It was time for me to stretch once again. Another friend of mine had recently launched a book and I noticed at the launch party how beautifully she spoke for over 30 minutes with only minimal notes. I called her to ask how she did that, and she connected me to her speaking coach.

Hiring a speaking coach was the best thing I ever did. She gave me the techniques I needed to get over my fears and pushed me to have a great opening. The audience decides if they like you in the first three seconds, she told me, so you need to come out strong. It was like grocery bag buyers, I thought, but a different nut to crack.

It took a couple of months of hard work and practice, but the speech went over well. The professor hosting the series said that, of the four speakers that year, I was the only female and the only one who didn't use PowerPoint. The feedback was very positive. The next day, I was asked to join the university's board of advisors known as the Corporation. For the next decade, I would serve as a Corporator, meet incredible friends, hear about groundbreaking research, and get energized at meetings that gave me insight into one of the most exciting and prestigious universities in the country.

Going to Boston from the Vineyard one fall to attend a meeting at Northeastern, I found myself on a plane with Bob Rosenberg of Dunkin' Donuts, the neighbor who had advised me to check the SBA site for my first business plan. Bob had retired from Dunkin' and was teaching business at Babson College, where he was going that day. He asked me how business was going, and I told him what I was doing, how sales were going, what my plans were. He listened and finally said, Wow, you're the real deal. You know, most people go to school for years to pull off what you're doing. It's fantastic.

I was pleased to hear his praise, but a little surprised. I felt in large part that success just happened to me. I was lucky to be in the right place at the right time. I felt all I did was solve the problems of the day. But I had to admit, I made good strategic choices, built solid relationships, took some bold chances that paid off, planned for and overcame a lot of obstacles, worked harder than I ever thought I could and, all in all, for a former English teacher, I had done pretty well.

# Chapter 12

# Mission Drift and Hubris

As my sales curve flattened, I began to be concerned about the long-term viability of 1 Bag at a Time. Where there had been no vendors of reusable bags in the US in 2005, suddenly after 2010, everyone seemed to be selling them. Watching the Kentucky Derby one day, my family and I were surprised to learn that a horse was being sponsored by a company I'd never heard of that claimed to be the leading vendor of reusable bags in the US. My friend who had introduced me to my freight forwarder and whose boss helped me with the reverse auction mentioned that her company was beginning to market and import reusable bags. I just wanted my piece of the pie, but I had a distinct feeling that my piece was getting smaller.

On top of that, I was beginning to feel that Gary was right. The details of selling reusable bags were pretty mundane. It was fun to build the business, but now in the flat part of the curve, taking orders and delivering product, there wasn't much challenge. The fire inside me dwindled to a smolder and my numbers were trending down. I started to think, *Now what?*

I didn't know how to manage this next phase of the business. Again, I turned to my network on Martha's Vineyard for advice. Talking it over with friends with far more business experience than I had, they all told me the same thing. There was no way to evade the long slow slog of commodities. Anyone could compete against me without much trouble. Customers would inevitably trickle away to lower-cost vendors.

The only way to have real long-term success is to build a brand, they said. I sort of thought I had a brand, but one of my friends set me straight. A commodity is not a brand. A brand, he said, is a company with a multi-tiered line of products, with brand barriers, sold in sustainable channels. I thought a lot about what he said. I had a multi-tiered line of products, and I was selling in sustainable channels. It was the phrase *brand barriers* that had me stumped.

This would be the start of two of the most exciting years for me in business and the two that would nearly lead me to lose it all. I made every classic mistake an entrepreneur can make, foremost among them, hubris and mission drift. As I embarked on creating my own brand, I would get caught up in the excitement of my own ideas, fail to take care of my core business, and end up overextended in ways that nearly ruined me. If ever there was a time when the lack of a business education affected my progress, this would be it. Then again, more than one MBA has fallen victim to hubris and mission drift. It's possible that, regardless of my education, I would need to learn this lesson the hard way.

Although my orders were going down, I was still near the top of my sales curve and had excellent reorder rates. During Expo West 2010, I found myself doing the same pitches, meeting the same people, and not feeling terribly energized. I was grateful to Sho and encouraging when larger clients came to the booth.

That year, probiotics were the new big thing. We were in a lifestyle aisle with other small, established brands. We were an easy aisle to skip, and a lot of buyers went right past us. The guy in the booth next to me, Kevin, was selling cat litter made from pine. We had plenty of time to chat. He was doing sales, but he really worked for the branding company and talked about branding a lot. Look, he said, anyone can chop up a pine tree to make cat litter. You need a brand to sell it.

Kevin's comment started me thinking. By being true to my values, principles, and mission, I did a lot of things right. I prioritized quality and ethics along my supply chain. I invested in tags that supported consumer education. I earned my place as a top bag supplier. I published op-eds, influenced legislators, and became a thought leader. I made good on my promises. Customers chose me for all these reasons, and 1 Bag at a Time was a good B2B (business-to-business) vendor. Still, I didn't have brand barriers and I wasn't a true brand. Toward the end of 2010, I called Kevin, reminded him of our chat about kitty litter and pine trees, and he referred me to his boss.

The first time I called him, I left a message. It went something like: Hi Bob, I met Kevin at Expo West last April and am thinking about branding a line of reusable tote bags. I've been selling reusable grocery bags for a few years and feel that there might be an opportunity for branding a line of bags of my own. Can you call me to discuss?

It took him a day or two to get back to me. As he would tell me later, he needed time to think about my request. As a branding opportunity, 99 cent grocery bags were not promising, was his first thought. They were usually an extension of other people's brands. Besides, usually product evolution worked the other way. A new product started out as a brand—an iconic dress or a designer bag—and then, within a few years, commodity traders would knock off designs and nearly everyone would have some version of that dress or handbag.

Then he started to think, *But why not tote bags?* His wife used reusable grocery bags for all kinds of things, and he used them for gym stuff occasionally. He started noticing that the women in his office were using them for extra shoes, lunch, and the like. How could a commodity bag maker take inspiration from, say, a $500 bag, or even a $5000 bag, and offer women everywhere a $5 solution? *It could be done*, he thought, and he called me back.

After a few conversations, he sent me a proposal. I told him I wanted a real brand, that is, a line of products with a look and feel I could build on. He said the first step was market research. That would mean a large survey of consumer attitudes toward bags—what people liked, didn't like, what they used them for, what they wanted. Also, a competitive review to see who else was out there offering bags at what prices. In early 2011, I signed a contract with him for a survey and competitive review. If we agreed there was further opportunity after the research, we would go on to engage in branding for a new line of bags.

The project gathered steam after the survey findings. The survey was aimed at women aged 18–55 who used reusable bags on a regular basis. Out of a thousand women contacted for the survey, 539 qualified, being within the gender and age range and self-identifying as using reusable bags regularly. The findings indicated that approximately 54% of women within the general population reported using reusable bags for 75% of their shopping trips. A few years later, other research would show that number to be 60% of women who saw themselves as reusable bag users, with higher numbers in many localities.[27]

That alone was validating. I remembered the buyer at Safeway telling me, a few years before, that 3% of their consumers used reusable bags, that the number had not changed since the 1970s. Here was proof that the number had changed! Reusable bag users were a majority among women even before widespread laws banning or taxing single-use bags. That was a huge win already!

The research also found:

- Consumers were using bags for 2.6 other uses beyond grocery.
- Half of consumers expressed willingness to pay more for a bag that did not advertise a grocery store or retailer, and over 90% chose *store logo* as what they least wanted to see on a purchased bag.
- Only 4% of women thought purchasing a shopping bag was too expensive, indicating that the overwhelming majority accepted the idea of purchasing bags.
- The average bag user owned seven bags, and those who said they were willing to pay more than $1 for a bag owned an average of ten bags.

The executive summary led with this:

> This panel validates the goals we set with 1 Bag at a Time at
> the Immersion session in early December 2010.
> By Earth Day 2012:
>
> - A multi-product Merchandising system in (2400 stores)
> - Average store sales of 3640/store = 10/day
> - A total Sales volume of 8–10MM bags = 8.7MM bags
> - The heart of the distribution strategy built around
>   success in 10 carefully selected mid-sized chains
> - An average unit cost to retailer of ($0.80)

From where I was, selling 8 million bags a year already, these
goals seemed ambitious but not impossible. If I met even half
those goals over the next couple of years, I would be happy.

We agreed we should take next steps. That meant me coming
to his offices in Charlotte, North Carolina for what he called a
blue sky exploration session.

The atmosphere was humming when I walked into the offices.
Bob met me at the door and ushered me into the conference
room. Kevin soon joined us along with a table full of others
from the office, those who wrote the survey and did competitive
research, those who were in product development, and others.
We spent the day talking about reusable bags.

Bob started the meeting saying that rarely was market
research so indicative of promise as the research on bags.
American women clearly not only accepted reusable shopping
bags, they embraced them and integrated them into many facets
of their lives. I flashed back to my first bags in Australia when
Gary and my daughters wanted bags of their own upon first
seeing them. Six years earlier, when I took the leap and started
selling bags during my fourth period break on the back staircase
of the English Department, I hoped fervently that others would

have the same experience I'd had. Now seeing what American women were telling us, my dream had come true. To think that I would be in North Carolina in a room full of people excited about giving American women what we started calling a bag of their own! I had come a long way.

Bob has a lot of experience in branding. I don't remember any of the exercises he took us through, but I do remember the way he inspired everyone to dig deep, be creative, generate idea after idea, throw out old thinking and invite new thinking in. His energy filled the room and we all responded. As the client and resident bag expert, I had the floor a lot of the time. Bob and I went back and forth on ideas in rapid succession, capturing phrases and suggestions on a whiteboard as we talked. Bob thought fast, spoke fast, generated ideas fast. Catching his energy, I started thinking just as fast, speaking just as fast, generating ideas just as fast. What was uncanny too is that Bob and I both have a similar vision disorder. We didn't talk about it, but anyone in the room couldn't help but notice that we each had one eye that tended inward and that we tilted our heads to the side to focus on someone. The day now to me is a blur, but I remember at the end of it overhearing two girls from the office remarking to each other: It's like they're twins or something! Clearly, we connected.

From there, we began a process of product development. Out of the dozens of names we came up with, the name that stuck was SnapSac. I bought SnapSac.com and, just for good measure, SnapSac.net and SnapSac.org and a few others just to ensure cyber-squatters didn't get too close. I was thinking about brand barriers.

Another lawyer friend told me that the patent office looked more favorably on individual trademark seekers than they did lawyers who applied for hundreds of trademarks a year. I applied for the trademark myself, working through the instructions on the US Patent and Trademark Office website.

The trademark was granted a few months later.

Bob's company created a brilliant branding brief, connecting everyday consumers who want it all—function, value, and fashion—to an upmarket, everyday bag. There was a pyramid of brand values, with the foundation being that the bag you carry is an extension of you, your style and your values. SnapSac would live up to the values, desires, and dreams of everyday American women.

Reading the branding brief, I thought back to my experience with Old Navy. When I first walked into their corporate offices, I passed three larger-than-life cutouts of ideal brand loyalists for Old Navy. On large boards in the lobby, smiling women beamed at me. I imagined how that must have felt to the people working there every day, designing, sourcing, and marketing sneakers, jeans, T-shirts and tote bags, remembering the people they really work for, the consumers they served.

I also remembered standing there in Old Navy, facing a wall with tote bags made by 1 Bag at a Time. Their positive messages of peace, hope, and love resonating with me as much as anyone else. I felt that SnapSac, the way we were envisioning it, could compete in this space, speak to the same demographic, help them express themselves in a simple everyday product. I didn't want to compete with Old Navy, far from it. SnapSac would be sold in grocery stores, maybe in the aisle with note cards and wrapping paper. Still, the Old Navy example reassured me that I wasn't kidding myself. There was a lot of evidence that a market for bags with more than a store logo existed if we could tap in. I felt we were on the right track.

Once we had a branding brief, Bob connected me to a designer to begin the process of branding and product design. I would work closely with this brilliant designer who was a perfect match for me and SnapSac. First, she absolutely crushed logo design. It was beautiful, elegant, memorable, everything I would want in a logo. In the center were two S letters reflecting each other, creating a negative space between that formed a heart. I loved it. Every time I saw it over the next few years, on my website, on my business card, on my email signature, it made me happy.

I found the designer to be attentive to market cues in ways that I had not considered. She looked at iconic bag brands, from luxury brands like Louis Vuitton and Gucci to mid-market brands like Longchamp and Coach, and distilled the design elements that made them beloved. First, they featured recognizable, geometric designs. Signature plaids and symmetry ruled. Second, they included features women loved, like pockets, closures, and zippers. Third, their most popular designs came in a variety of sizes—the same shape, but different sizes for different uses. Together, we agreed these elements would govern the development of SnapSac.

**smart.**
**stylish.**
**shopping.**

She came through with a fantastic design for a range of bags, an all-purpose foldable tote in three sizes, an insulated lunch tote, an insulated large grocery/picnic tote, and a foldable grocery tote. All of them had a signature diamond-shaped flap at the top that snapped closed, the snap in SnapSac. They folded up into a tiny rectangle, and unfolded into a variety of sizes, one that easily fit a shoebox or lunch, another that fit a change of clothes for the gym, and a MegaTote, an enormous tote that would fit everything you might want to take along with your kids for an overnight at the grandparents' house. Secretly, the MegaTote was my favorite. It looked enormous but easily tucked under your arm.

We decided that the marketing would feature as many alliterative S-words as possible. My background in poetry came in handy as I began marketing in earnest. Later my weekly SnapSac emails would be filled with the rhetorical devices I'd learned and taught in English classes: alliteration, balanced sentences, parallelism, assonance, enjambment, meter. There's nothing like poetry if you want to say something clever and memorable in the fewest words possible.

The designer also came through with a geometric design based on dots and developed exciting color combinations for each item. It was a beautiful realization of the vision—I think far better than either Bob or I imagined. We both got excited. Maybe too excited now that I look back, but they were really beautiful for a five-dollar bag.

The next step was to get samples made and test them out. I had been telling Amy that I was developing new items, and even she was surprised and delighted at the variety and innovation. I sent her patterns and the factory sent back lovely sample bags. There were a few modifications I wanted after I got my  first samples to improve durability, like sewing handles to the bottom of the bag. Because the MegaTote was so large, I insisted on double fabric for increased strength. I approved the items in June, and we would get the first product in September 2011.

Meanwhile, I was preparing marketing materials for SnapSac. I met a trade-show designer at Expo West that I liked, named Jim. He and his team were fantastic—talented, creative, visionary. They created letterhead and business cards, and the most amazing brochure and images I'd ever seen. The central photo was a professional woman in a white dress and red sandals running through a plaza in a city that looked like Rome, trailing a SnapSac PetiteTote. The brochure itself folded up into a little triangle like the triangular snap-closure flap on the bag. Brilliant! They gave me images I would use on the website and sales materials.

Jim and his team would also create a beautifully branded booth for SnapSac at Expo West 2012. I hired Ciplex to create the website and they knocked it out of the park. I even hired a PR firm to get magazine press. They wrote a press release and coordinated a full press launch.

No doubt, it was all incredibly empowering and exciting to build this team and inspire them to support this vision. I would

learn later to be more careful about my enthusiasm. I would learn the hard way to listen for skepticism like the little hesitation that I'd heard in Bob's first conversation with me. As a paying client, I drove a lot of decisions forward and I can see now that if they had doubts, it was not in their best interest to bring them to me. If they gently suggested something, it was up to me to listen, and I'll admit, I was carried away in large part by my own excitement. I really had done my research. I really did believe there was an opportunity there. I would soon find a lot of early success both in sales and press coverage that validated the research and excitement. I wasn't the only one excited, but truth be told, no one got excited until they heard from me.

I targeted Sprouts as my first client for SnapSac and created a killer trade deck. I used everything I knew from teaching persuasive arguments—the logical, rhetorical, and emotional tools that I'd studied and that worked from time immemorial. Everything I learned from consumer research, all the color spotting and competitive market research that had gone into SnapSac. Everything I learned about business analysis to make a case about the market share of bags leaking out of grocery stores (Old Navy for example) and the opportunity to win some of that back, and always the convincing science that reusable bags were best and aligned with strong consumer desire to be eco-friendly. I showcased my ideal SnapSac consumer so buyers could visualize and get to know the woman who wanted a bag of her own. I worked hard to create a visually pleasing layout, uncluttered, with very clear messaging on each card, inexorably leading to the conclusion that this product was the right product for this moment. As an argument, it was watertight, and it worked.

I went to see Susan at Sprouts in Arizona. She was no longer the bag buyer but attended with the new buyer who reported up to her. I presented the research, the need, and the product: SnapSac, for women who wanted a bag of their own for about five bucks. I unveiled the product line and pricing. I explained my go-to-market strategy. I gave them samples. They were very pleased, took samples, talked about launching in early 2012, and said they'd think about it for a few days. They did and then called me to accept. We started working out the details of a product rollout for a hundred stores, the support I would offer, and the mix of products for each store.

About this time, Bob started pressuring me to hire Kevin as a sales rep for SnapSac. I couldn't do all the sales myself, he said, and Kevin had established relationships with buyers. I was limiting myself if I didn't have a rep in the field.

It was a pricey contract with a lot of guaranteed payment. I was reluctant, already having spent a lot of money in bag development and the launch. I didn't have the experience at the time to insist on a 100% commission model, which I should have done, or at least high commission. In the end, I trusted Bob. He was a consumer product goods specialist. He knew his clients and the industry. I resisted for a few weeks, but he was insistent. Finally, I gave in.

It was late fall 2011 and we were planning for Expo West 2012. I upgraded to a double booth with a simple, appealing design. The SnapSac avatars were larger than life on the backdrop.

In early 2012, it was all coming together. The PR team landed a feature in *Good Housekeeping* that generated a ton of sales on my website. We had given bags away at a few celebrity events and had photos of celebs posing with SnapSac. I ordered about 20,000 bags in total in different styles and sizes for promotions, selling, and for Sprouts.

From my experience with 1 Bag at a Time when we hit the hockey-stick curve, I knew I had lost clients due to my inability to deliver product on time. I was dedicated to not making the same mistake twice, so I started planning reorders early. As it would turn out, my experience wasn't a very good guide in this case. Six years before, when I launched 1 Bag at a Time, indicators were against me. People were advising me not to do it—there was no market for it, Americans would not reuse bags—and yet, I hit a hockey-stick curve. Now, all indications were go. I was entering an ancillary market that was proven in other channels. All my research, my PR, my early sales, and my team were validating a full push ahead.

Somewhere in January, Amy and I decided I should place the next purchase orders early so she could take delivery of fabric before Chinese New Year. That way, we could move directly into cutting, printing, and sewing after the holidays to push up production schedules. It would be a push to get product in late April, but if we had fabric, it could be done. I prepared purchase orders and doubled the quantity. I purchased a used forklift and installed warehouse racks.

Andrea, my assistant, asked if I was a little early in ordering, and suggested we might want to order fewer bags. I dismissed her criticism. She shook her head and went back to her desk. The purchase orders went out. We wouldn't get them until April, after Expo West and after spring sales. I was confident we would need them.

This time for Expo West, we had a fully-fledged plan. I paid to have press kits available for journalists, which gave me a ticket to a press event the night before the doors opened. Press kits included a shot of our feature in *Good Housekeeping* and shots of celebrities with SnapSac. On the floor on Friday, Saturday, and Sunday, we scheduled how many bags we would hand out and when. On Friday, we would hand out MegaTotes, the largest totes we had, which were perfect for a trade show.

As soon as we started giving out bags, we were mobbed. For three days straight, we had a crowd five to eight people deep waiting to be scanned, pitched, and given a bag. All over the floor, women were wandering around with the MegaTote, and other women were asking where to get one. We gave out 200 to 300 a day and there were a lot more takers, but we had a limit. People who came after we ran out of samples got scanned and were told to come back tomorrow.

Sometime during that crazy weekend, when we were out of bags, two women came up to my booth and introduced themselves as the new product team from Target. We had a long chat, they got bags and a press kit, and we set up a time to follow up the next week. Not long afterwards, a guy came up to me from Costco.

It was three days of insanity, and I hardly knew where I was after it. I had orders for my regular customers coming in that needed processing. Sprouts launched the product in late March or early April. PR and press mentions continued to come in.

In spite of all these good indications, sometime in April I began to get early intimations of trouble. Sprouts reported that the bags weren't selling as well as expected.

The buyer wanted to know when the display rack was coming in. I ordered enough racks for all 100 Sprouts stores, but they were behind schedule. Apparently, customers didn't know what the folded items were. Some people were unfolding them and leaving them on the floor. Thinking it through later, I remembered discussing displays with Bob at some point. How would people know what size they were or what they were for? We discussed options, but we never decided anything, and the rack I ordered was a simple one.

Looking back, not having a merchandising system was a key omission in our strategy. Every time people saw what the product was for, they wanted one. Folded up in a grocery store, it was not flying off the shelf.

Meanwhile, other signs continued to show that we had hit a mark. I got a call from *Good Morning America* in response to our press kit. Did SnapSac want to be featured on their Deals and Steals segment?

Yes, we did! I worked directly with Tory Johnson's team. I contracted with their recommended website vendor to create a dedicated *GMA* site with a few different options for bag packages. Apparently, GMA deals generated huge traffic and most normal sites would crash. The show got a stack of totes for their on-camera demonstration. Robin Roberts and Lara Spenser would both be shown trying them out and chatting about how cute and useful they were.

The pace of this promotion was fast and furious. We had less than two weeks to get the site and promotional packages ready. The segments aired on Thursday April 19, right around Earth Day. I was told to stand by, starting at 5 a.m., with the first segment airing sometime in the 8 a.m. hour on the East Coast. Up with the sun, I sat and watched the orders as they came in. By the end of the day, we'd sold over 40,000 SnapSac items out of our warehouse, about 10,000 orders of four bags each, directly to consumers. It was a huge win and an unbelievable promotional opportunity for SnapSac. It was also 10,000 more emails to add to our marketing list.

The next day, I sat down with my staff to work out details of how to get 40,000 bags to consumers in small orders. A couple of days later, the web team sent us a spreadsheet with details of all our orders, which we imported into QuickBooks. Andrea and I produced stacks of labels clipped to packing lists within a couple of days and collected them in bankers' boxes for warehouse processing.

At the end of the week, we hired eight temps to pick and pack. Shannon and Sho checked every envelope for accuracy. Mistakes would be costly. Between the site and cost of temps and postage, there was little margin for error. Packages that were accurate were sealed, labeled, and put in large bins near the loading dock for pickup. Those with pick-and-pack errors were given back to a temp to try again. Our mail carrier was fantastic, helping us arrange for trucks all week to pick up thousands of bags. All told, the operation went off flawlessly and we had a huge PR success. There were remarkably few complaints. Tory Johnson would call two or three times later that year to feature us again. The response was always great, and she loved working with us.

Slowly I would come to the realization that in spite of all the research, in spite of all the product development, in spite of the shared enthusiasm across a team of experts, in spite of early enthusiasm by buyers and consumers from *Good Housekeeping*, Expo West, *Good Morning America*, Sprouts, and many others, there were no reorders at all.

As more purchase orders were beginning to ship from China in the late spring of 2012, I asked Amy to slow things down. She tried to accommodate me as much as possible. Factories too had limited space. My warehouse was small, and I knew there was no room for another container of SnapSacs.

What's more, my focus on SnapSac had taken away my focus from my core business, reusable grocery bags. As I asked Sho to pick up the slack, I found he was less successful with large clients. It wasn't his fault, it was mine. He had always been in charge of small orders. I trained him in the early years for that, and I didn't invest the time and training needed for him to handle larger orders. As the sales curve flattened, it really flattened. I couldn't count on 1 Bag at a Time to make up for the cash-flow problems that SnapSac was posing. As summer wore on, it was starting to dawn on me that it might not just be a cash-flow problem. I might incur real losses.

Andrea's head-shaking return to her desk that day when I placed reorders was an image that I replayed often in my head. It was a classic moment of my own hubris. I forgot my core mission—saving the world 1 Bag at a Time—and overinvested in a new, untried, and untested concept that ultimately failed. Every entrepreneur fails. The saying goes, Fail fast, fail early. I failed at the height of my momentum. Probably, I failed too late. Whatever it was about, SnapSac was not about the moral imperative that drove my early success. Problems mounted as fall moved into winter. I still had product in China that Amy was pressuring me to ship. My cash was dwindling even as my revenue was falling.

There's no need to go into the list of mistakes I made. I needed to turn things around. I started pulling back expenses hard. From now on, nothing went out if it wasn't bringing something in.

One of the first things to go was the contract paying Kevin as a sales representative. In all the months I was paying him, Kevin didn't sell one bag. It was disappointing to say the least. I never liked the sales deal to begin with and should have trusted my instincts. I was afraid Bob would insist on the contract, but he caved in easily and let me out of it. That was when I knew that he knew he'd overreached. Maybe I should have asked for money back, but I didn't want to talk to him any more than I had to. I had bigger fish to fry.

I also got serious about collecting on debts. Sprouts used a local Southern California distributor. Back in early summer, when SnapSac didn't sell as planned, a buyer from the distributor emailed to ask me to take back what they'd ordered. I told them that I didn't have a buyback agreement with either them or Sprouts.

In a nasty move, the distributor then put in two purchase orders for container loads of grocery bags with the Sprouts logo on them — their usual bag that we sold for years. I delivered those two containers in July, and by September they still refused to pay. Besides the SnapSac problems, now I had two more containers of bags that I had paid for and didn't have cash flow on. As the fall went on, it was clear that the distributor was withholding payment on these private-label orders amounting to nearly six figures in order to pressure me to take back SnapSac. All their accounting department said was that my account was on hold.

My experience collecting what people owed me served me well. I tried to escalate the issue to people who were decision makers. There was no use hammering anyone on the front line. However, I couldn't get anyone very high up on the phone. One day, I drove to their offices in Orange County and dropped in on my buyer, Maria. As I was unexpected, the receptionist took me in to see her. Maria was visibly flustered. I showed her copies of her purchase orders and asked her what we needed to do to get them paid. She was texting under her desk and furiously writing emails as I was there, no doubt to her superiors asking what to do. I'm pretty sure she was told to stonewall, which she did. She wasn't the decision maker, and I didn't make her the brunt of any anger. I tried to get to her boss but was refused. A purchase order is a contract, I said, and they were in breach. I let her know that if they didn't pay, they could explain it to a judge as I would sue them.

The last thing I wanted was to engage a lawyer. Lawyers' fees would eat half or more of what they owed me. At this point, though, it was clear that I wasn't going to get anything from them unless I forced their hand, so I started to reconcile myself to going to court in the hope of getting half. I let them know I was engaging counsel and got a flurry of emails. I was very clear that I would seek to make them pay a lot more than their purchase orders if I took them to court. Trying to hold me over a barrel for customized bags that were of no use to anyone else was not just a nasty tactic, it was illegal. I would sue for interest and damages.

When they realized I was serious, they backed down and issued payment. Being willing to sue them seemed to be enough and, thankfully, I didn't have to file suit. Throughout this fight, I tried to keep my buyer at Sprouts out of the dispute, but somehow he got wind of it. He apologized and I told him it wasn't his fault. He agreed to tell the distributor that he would work with them to sell through the merchandise and not try to return it to me. I thanked him. Although it all worked out, the next year Sprouts changed bag vendors and I lost a major client. I knew I deserved it. Hubris and mission drift. I learned these lessons the hard way.

For the most part, Andrea and I had an excellent working relationship. We loved a Starbucks in the mid-morning and either she or I would take a quick trip for coffees, and I was always happy to pay. She was well compensated, and I made sure she had the technology and tools she needed to do her job. One day in mid-November, Andrea came into my office. She had gotten us both coffees, for which I was grateful.

I need to tell you something, she started. I'm giving you notice. I've accepted another job.

I was in shock. We worked together every day. Did I miss the signs that she was unhappy? Had I offended or let her down in some way? There was a deep silence between us. I knew Andrea kept her personal life very separate from work, which was fine. She was an assistant. To her, this was just a job. Finally, I said okay. There was nothing else to say. I wished her well and asked her to discuss her plans with me the next day about how she could prepare for the next person to take her place.

When Dante enters the gates of hell, the inscription reads: Abandon all hope, ye who enter here. As Andrea walked out, I felt as though I now was certainly passing through the gates of my own personal hell. What lay before me was dark and unknown. I started to think this was disaster upon disaster.

Mostly, Andrea was in charge of accounts payable, accounts receivable, and other routine bookkeeping tasks like bank reconciliations, which I didn't want to do and didn't have the patience for. Andrea had taken vacations regularly and had put together some basic instructions about how to do her job while she was away. Now she set about updating them as training materials to leave behind. As I started thinking about the job she did for me, I figured she had seen the numbers and lost faith that the company would survive. She was jumping ship.

It was a dark week for me. Andrea's lack of faith shook me. Even when I started cutting my salary, I had protected her, Sho, and Shannon. Now I stopped to wonder, who was working for whom? Andrea's departure revealed all the problems with where I was at the time. I had taught myself how to acquire and maintain key accounts, but I had not trained or mentored any of my employees to take on serious income-producing roles. They all supported me, which was fine when I was producing high levels of sales. When sales fell, the business model began to break down.

Even as early as September, I had let Sho know that I expected him to work nearly full-time on SnapSac, which he didn't want to do. He never saw the appeal. Now, I doubled down. With Andrea's impending departure, I let him know that it would be SnapSac all the time, and if he didn't have his heart in it, he might want to consider a job elsewhere. Eventually, he did just that. It was a difficult process for me, but I knew he had stagnated, and I could no longer help him grow. It was in his best interest as well as mine.

When Andrea left, I took up her instructions and tried to see if I could do what she did. The worst part was the merchant reconciliations from our online sales. Although our margin was much higher direct to consumer, it was a complex business to figure out web-orders for the week, get them into QuickBooks accurately, adjust inventory, record the credit card fees correctly, and then reconcile them against what the credit card company was putting in my bank account. I wondered if I could automate that process somehow.

Enter CartSpan, the brainchild of Scott Wheeler. Scott is a coder who had written a plugin that connected my site to my QuickBooks. From the *Good Morning America* sales, I knew that once customer and order data was in QuickBooks, I could generate an invoice and a label in a click or two and record payment accurately. CartSpan was the connection I needed. Reconciliations were accurate and easy after that.

When I called Scott and asked him to walk me through the integration process, he was more than happy to help. I paid $800 for a year of CartSpan, and he was a really cheerful tech support agent for the first few weeks while I got it set up and learned to use it. Alone in my office those first few weeks, a call to Scott often brightened my day.

Within a month of Andrea's leaving, I realized that I could take over most of her duties pretty easily. It was a little shocking to find that I could replace such a valued employee with an $800 app. I didn't like bank reconciliations, and still don't, but once all my transactions were properly imported, it wasn't impossible. I started reconciling religiously every month. Having my expenses stare me in the face month after month helped me become more careful about my spending and focused me once again on cash flow, that not-to-be-neglected talisman of good financial decisions.

By the end of December, Sho found another job and I was down to one employee, Shannon. I was figuring out how to get by with less. The distributor finally paid. I was no longer in a downward spiral, but I was in a pretty deep hole. I was six figures into debt with Amy. My rent was too high with almost a year still on my lease. I had too much unsold inventory, my revenues were falling, and I still needed payroll for Shannon. I had my own loading dock and forklift! What was I thinking! I had never wanted to be in the warehouse business.

As the holidays came, I found myself in a deep depression, unable to sleep, deeply regretful and aware of my own mistakes, and ruminating over my worst moments. I showed up at family gatherings, but really, I wasn't there. I couldn't share in the happiness of those around me. I did my best to smile and hide it. There was no one to share my problems with. I hinted at problems with Gary, and he didn't want to hear about it. He trusted me to figure it out. I hadn't taken a salary since September and wasn't sure I could survive this.

The closer the holidays came, the more I lost sight of what had driven me into the business. All the energy and drive that characterized my early years was gone. I had let people down along my whole supply chain, and that failure, more than anything else, weighed on me. I spent weeks in what felt like a black hole, beating myself up, unable to think about how to get out. I went through the motions of business and life, keeping my head up and feeling that at any moment, I would lose my footing and fall, disgraced, forever. If before I had stepped through a looking glass, this time I fell down the rabbit hole. It was a long way down.

# Chapter 13

# Exit Strategy

Midway on that journey, I lost my way.

That's the first line of Dante's *Inferno*, the initial act that precipitates his descent into Hades. That's exactly how I felt. I saw that as I pursued SnapSac, I lost my way, strayed from the mission that guided me through my first years—saving the world 1 Bag at a Time. Dante understood that wandering is part of human nature and that many of us find ourselves in some kind of wilderness, descending into a dark place and frightful place. At some point, we have to do some deep soul-searching to find the right path back.

After weeks of self-recrimination, I found myself with more questions than answers. Why did SnapSac fail? Did I misjudge the market or was there something wrong with the product? What was I doing with a forklift? Why hadn't Andrea made a case for me to slow down? Why did Sho never learn to develop larger contracts?

I'd had bosses who hadn't listened, bosses who threatened to fire me when my family needed me, bosses who said: Don't let the door hit you on the way out. I had gone out of my way to be a good boss, to make space for my employees to talk to me, to be empathetic, to show concern for their health and help them balance their lives, to give them new experiences and help them grow new skills. This was particularly true with Sho, whom I had hired to pick and pack and whom I trained to listen to customers and speak carefully to them, to know the answers to their questions before they asked. He learned so much in his early years and at Expo West. Why did he stop growing? Was I a bad boss?

For 1 Bag at a Time, I did everything myself—the marketing,

the branding, the sales, the supply chain and logistics—and it worked. What did I do wrong when I looked to go beyond my own abilities to build a team of experts, people with excellent skills, knowledge, and experience? Why did none of them see the failure coming? How had I let them push me so far? Had I been the one pushing them?

I have always, since my early days, been brutally honest with myself. I can't grow if I can't face my failings and overcome them. Here now, I really had to come to terms with what I didn't know. Much later, as a coach, I would spend my first year acquiring the knowledge that I was missing, learning how to develop leadership in others, what to look for in an interview, how to encourage people to grow and stretch. At that time, I had never heard of business coaching. Later I would wish I had.

*I can't grow if I can't face my failings and overcome them.*

For now, I was still passionate about reusable bags being better for sustainability, better for consumers, and better for business. I was still good at sales and managing key accounts. I was still good at supply chain logistics. I still knew how to tell a good story, how to create a memorable piece of marketing, how to listen and empathize with potential customers and offer solutions to their problems, how to inspire others and energize them to be part of a better future that I could help them envision. I would have to rely on all those strengths like never before to climb out of this mess, and that's what I set out to do.

There was no moment when I started to rise up out of the circles of hell that I had fallen into, no jolt of realization, no hand that helped me up. There was just a new day every morning, and when the holidays were over, there was an office to go to. Showing up gave me the space I needed to figure out how to move forward. I stopped blaming myself and started tapping into my inner resources and instincts. If I had come this far, I could finish this. I wasn't a quitter, even when faced with a bunch of pig shit. Solve the problems of the day—that was all I needed to do. It was all I could do. So, that's what I did.

First and foremost, I had to deal with Amy. Over Skype late one night, I came clean about not being able to pay for all the inventory I had ordered. In particular, there were some 7000 CoolTotes, our most expensive item, the one with the highest duty rate and most costly for shipping. I wasn't sure I could sell them at a profit. Amy was extraordinarily gracious and understanding. I had been a driver of much of her success over recent years, and she was in a strong position. I told her that I needed to cut my losses and ask the factory to destroy the product in China. She balked at first, and finally agreed. She understood. She also agreed to pay the factories for me and allow me to pay her off over time. Those two first steps took a huge weight off my shoulders, and I was forever grateful for Amy's friendship and support at that moment.

The next step was to get out of my lease. I was now quite clear that I had never wanted to be in the warehouse business, and I had to get out. When I first met with the landlord, he insisted there was no exit option. I shifted into persuasive mode very quickly. I don't remember what I said. I just know that I was charming, sincere, open about my troubles, and did my best to appeal to his sense of decency as a person. In the end, he let me out of the lease in March, two months from then, saving me about eight months of rent that I could no longer afford.

Shannon and I cleared things out. I got rid of a bunch of inventory to a clearance broker, someone who profits when vendors like me go belly-up. It was no consolation to learn that my plight was common enough to fuel an industry of its own. I was selling at a loss, but the point was no longer to make a profit. I had to cut my losses. I sold the forklift and paid off the loan for it. The landlord found a new tenant who bought my

Ikea office furniture for a few hundred bucks, which kept me from having to junk them or deal with Craigslist. In the end, we had a few thousand grocery bags and fewer than 5000 SnapSac bags that I transferred back to Jim's third-party warehouse. Jim was glad to have me back. I was more than relieved to be back. The only thing I was sorry for was having to let Shannon go. I wished I could have done better for him. He was sorry he couldn't do more for me. It was my fault, I assured him. The last day was a sad one.

That night, Gary took me out to dinner. I ordered a martini, which I almost never do. I'm a lightweight and a glass of wine or two is as much as I can usually take. I could see my way out now. I had no employees, no rent, and paid only for the warehouse space and services I needed. I would pay Amy off over time and dedicate myself to selling reusable grocery bags, taking care of my clients, and getting serious about business. I would have to hit sales targets. If that meant going back to cold calling, so be it. I would lock down expenses. I would cancel my trip to China. No more mission drift, no more hubris, just buckling down to sell the bags with my customers' logos on them, day after day.

In the middle of dinner I excused myself, went to the bathroom, and had myself a good cry. I still loved my business and didn't mind getting serious. It was the thought of sitting home alone with no office to go to—no one to talk to about bags, shipping, logos, and the topics of the day—that was terrifying and lonely. It was the only way out. I could see the plan and envision becoming profitable and stable as a business again, but this would be the hardest phase of my business.

Later, as I embarked on my next career as a business coach, I was hungry to understand more about where I went wrong. After my coach training, I would invest time and money acquiring expertise in HR—hiring, managing, and leadership development—and would come to understand how I'd failed as a manager and a boss. On my own, I had picked up how to sell, how to market, how to build a supply chain and a logistics team, how to manage cash flow. I thought my staff would grow the way I did—naturally, on their own—but I realized I didn't give them the experiences or challenges they would need to grow. I was too wrapped up in my own growth, pushing boundaries until I pushed too far and found the edge.

I found myself gravitating to material about failure. Conan O'Brien's commencement speech at Dartmouth College resonated deeply with me. Much later, reading my friend Bob Rosenberg's memoir, *Around the Corner to Around the World*, about how he built Dunkin' Donuts into a publicly owned doughnut empire, what stood out for me was his admission of succumbing to hubris and mission drift, and his ability to own that time with humility and honesty.

Through that book, I would be led to Daniel Halberstam's *The Best and the Brightest*, a monumental tale of mission drift and hubris which would give me the inspiration to write this book. Halberstam's prose turned nonfiction into art. In the same way that I read the Greek tragedies or *Anna Karenina*, I read every word, admired every sentence, the tone and scope and the sheer feat of what Halberstam pulled off. Turning to write my own story, I would read Halberstam nonstop for months. If you're going to try to be something, you might as well try to be the best.

As I came to terms with my failures and worked hard to make good again on my promises, I recovered my happiness and was able to find my still-deep belief in reusable bags. By now, it was 2013, and business had shifted from phones to email. It took all my writing skills to convey my passion for bags in an email. I wrote sales replies carefully, took time to individualize messages and answer questions fully.

Sometimes there were days when I never once talked to a person. Orders were still strong, and my reorder rate was stable. I hit my sales targets, paid off my debts, and started becoming profitable again. I was living my values and that kept me going day after day. While I terribly missed having colleagues, I discovered some silver linings about working from home. By this time, Gary and I were empty nesters. Taking an hour at lunch to put together a dinner that would simmer on the stove made it easy to have a delicious and easy dinner later on. Taking breaks to have coffee and put a load of washing in the machine kept me from doing laundry at all hours of the night. Wearing sweats to work. Avoiding LA traffic. These are things many of us would discover later in the pandemic, but that had been my new normal for years before the arrival of Covid-19. Still, these benefits were not full compensation for the social rewards of life in an office.

Taking over my own operations and logistics, I discovered an even more efficient process for keeping trucking costs under control. I always pushed my warehouse staff to get bids on every load, every week, but I found resistance. My warehouse staff wasn't drawn to intricate spreadsheets the way I was. Now as I look back, I realize I hadn't hired people who were drawn to spreadsheets. Left to do it myself, I developed a tight bidding system, with a complex Excel form detailing each order and where it had to go. Every week, I sent the form out to three different freight brokers to bid on each load. I had a separate sheet to record bids and choose the winner.

I maintained good relationships with all my freight brokers, but I didn't allow myself to play favorites. The guy with the lowest bid got the load. Freight brokers learned that they couldn't win my business by charging up too much. Still, I had a lot of business and they wanted it. I used to joke with them that everyone on my supply chain got to eat, but no one was getting fat. I worked only with brokers who were reliable and tracked my freight. As my shipping rates got tighter, my profits went up. It was another piece of the puzzle of bringing my business back to profitability in the cutthroat world of commodities.

One day, as my new routine began to gel, I got a surprise email from Stan at Earthwise Bags. Would I want to sell 1 Bag at a Time to him? I figured that his sales curve was flattening too, and that he was thinking an acquisition would bolster sales. At any other time, I would have said no as politely and quickly as possible. But now, I could see the advantage of offloading responsibility for cash flow. I agreed to meet Stan at his offices in Burbank. A friend of mine who was a mergers and acquisitions lawyer cautioned me to listen more than I spoke, which was good advice.

A South African native, Stan is a tall guy, over 6 feet, who started importing garments in Los Angeles in the 1970s. He towered over me physically and had decades of experience on me. Stan was complimentary but let me know he regarded my company as a small acquisition. He sounded me out and I gave him a rough idea of the volume I was doing, careful to speak in generalities like the average number of containers I had coming in each week. He was interested in my accounts in the hardware industry, where he had not made much progress at all, probably because I was dominant there. We both decided to think about it.

The next week he made me an offer. It was a modest offer and included me working for him as a sales rep for a year. It would take a lot out of me to work for him, I knew, but there was something attractive about having a pile of cash, even if it was a small pile of cash, having colleagues, and being free of carrying a whole business on my own shoulders. It was essentially what I made in a year. Because I would have to work for him, it wasn't much of a payoff. Then again, I wasn't sure there would ever be a payoff, so I considered it. I knew this might be the best offer I would ever get.

I discussed my quality-control processes with Stan, and he wasn't impressed. He was clear that all product would come from his supplier, not mine. He was more interested in volume than quality. I explained that my customers were used to a certain quality bag and might look for other vendors if they didn't like the new bag. He said customers didn't care much about quality and he wasn't concerned.

I searched deep in my heart to see if I could work with someone who didn't care about quality, if I could leave Amy like that, if I had what it would take to bite my tongue and not disagree with Stan, to take a demotion and become a sales rep reporting to him. I wasn't sure I could. For a few months, maybe, but for a year? In the end, I told Stan thanks, but I wanted to keep my slice of the pie. I'd carved out a nice little piece and I was happy with what I had.

But the seed was planted. Could I sell my company? What was it worth? How long did I want to stay home and sell bags in a room by myself? How could I get what I wanted? For that matter, what did I want? Could I get someone to buy it and run it the way I had, with the supply chain and competitive advantages of quality and ethics that were the foundation of my business and that spoke to my clientele?

I wasn't sure how to go about getting answers. I asked around, and my accountant referred me to a business brokerage, where I was connected to Patricia, a broker who had the answers I was looking for. To find a selling price, she took the last three years of my tax returns, calculated my average profit, and then there was a multiplier. For a commodity company like mine, the multiplier was two or maybe two and a half times the annual profit. They would average my numbers for the last three years, count as profit any expenses that were personal like phone bills and travel expenses, apply the multiplier, and that would give me the selling price.

That was exactly what I needed to know. If I could sell the company for two to three times my annual average profits, that gave me a few years to figure out what else I wanted to do. My tax return for the year before was a complete disaster. I knew I would have to be profitable for at least three years. Still, 2013 wasn't a bad year and I thought I could do better in 2014. I decided to do a refresh on my website and work harder at SEO and internet marketing. I would have to control expenses and grow sales for at least two more years, but I had a shot. The idea of selling was a motivating factor for me over the next couple of years. I didn't have the heart to commit long term to sitting in a home office selling grocery bags, but I could do it short term if there was a bigger goal—an exit strategy. It would be rough, but I could be disciplined. I was still learning accounting and finding it more interesting than I thought it would be. I learned that the numbers told the story of what was happening, and I liked stories. Also, I decided: I needed a puppy.

It would take me nearly a year to get the puppy I wanted, but the search and thought of it kept me going as I hunkered down to a routine that was very home-bound, repetitive, and focused. I attended to my key accounts, ensured they had the artwork and products they needed. I reached out to former clients to see what bag needs I could help with. I redoubled my efforts at marketing, using the email marketing lists I had grown. Ciplex was no longer around but I found a good designer and worked to get the site updated.

Over the next few years, I worked on becoming a real business. I kept expenses lean and mean. Everything that could be more efficient was. The more I was involved in my own books, the better I got at making sure I was getting returns for my investments. Business was, as it always had been, about cash flow. I spent serious time in business analysis, profit/loss sheets, balance sheets, future-cash-flow projections, knowing where I wanted to go and executing on plan. I started paying myself again and worked to increase profits, which I did for three years in a row.

I got my puppy and he kept me company, made sure I got out a few times a day to walk and smell fresh air. I would have many days when I talked to no one but the dog. On those days, as soon as Gary came home, I would ask him to take me out, just wanting to be in a room with other people even if it was a restaurant. It was a lonely few years, but I became happy in the progress I was making, held myself accountable to strict goals, watched cash flow sharply, and understood better how to control and grow a business with discipline. This time it wasn't a lucky fluke. It was the hard work of day-to-day sales and operations management.

It was 2016 when I reached out to Patricia again to put the business up for sale. Patricia dug into the details, looking at three profitable years of tax returns and valuating my business. The first thing she did was recast my profit/loss sheet as reported on my tax statements into a statement of Seller's Discretionary Earnings. I wasn't sure what that was, but the subtitle read: Also called Adjusted Net Income or Cash Flow. Cash flow was an old friend. My cash flow is what the multiplier would be based on. I imagine Patricia could hear me exhale when I saw it. I was thankful I had been disciplined. I was ready to sell.

Patricia started with basics—seller's permits, corporate documents, and the like. Once she confirmed I had proper legal standing, she started asking about who my customers were, who my suppliers *Cash flow was an old friend.* were, and what my competitive advantages were. After so many years of working alone, it was a relief to talk to someone about my work. We spent long hours on the phone and sent many emails back and forth. I had questions for Patricia too.

Who bought businesses like this?

Often, she said, it was someone who could afford to buy themselves a job, solopreneurs. They like the autonomy of working from home, calling their own shots, working flexibly when they want to work according to their own needs.

How long did it take?

It's like selling a house—as long as it takes to find a buyer willing to give you an offer you'll accept.

How do we explain what I have without giving away what makes my company valuable? I was mindful of my lack of brand barriers.

Patricia said her company used a confidential business review process, starting with a non-disclosure agreement. She would work with me to create a document about the business that showed its advantages without disclosing any proprietary knowledge. With that, Patricia and I embarked on a six-month process resulting in a 40-page document that would be the basis of buyer offers.

After the wild ride of the hockey-stick curve and the lost years of mission drift, I discovered that what was ultimately most valuable were the unglamorous, often tedious and lonely years of buckling down to stabilize the business and create a history of profitability and positive cash flow. Certainly, the foundation I built in my early years supported the business model. My brand focus on quality and ethics resonated with my customers and generated a lot of loyalty. The strong, stable supply chain became another competitive advantage, a plug-and-play solution for reliable and economically priced inventory. Without profitability, none of that mattered, but with a steady cash flow, Patricia assured me I had something to sell. Additionally, the company had a nice inspirational and environmental message. She was sure that the company would have a lot of appeal.

The difficult part of pricing was the flow of goods. Year-over-year profitability and value was easier to establish than the price of the company at any one moment. I constantly had orders in production, orders in transit, and accounts receivable. Because I was dealing with container loads of product, the price of any of these elements could fluctuate up to six figures on any one day. Eventually we broke down how the deal would go. It was complicated, but the formula made sense.

We first put information about the business on the market in August 2016. We received a lot of inquiries, a husband-and-wife team from North Carolina, a woman from the Chicago area, and others with serious questions. By October, there was no offer. Eager to sell, I agreed to lower the asking price by $50,000. It was still good money, and I was going on year four of sitting home alone. At this point, I was committed to selling, and I knew a lot about sales. A lower price raised my positioning, and I still didn't have to take any offer I didn't like.

During that time, Patricia was a bright spot in my days. I felt she was on my team, and I was grateful to have someone to talk to about how things were going. Later, as a coach, I knew how valuable it was to have a trusted advisor to talk to about the issues of the day, to celebrate the little wins, to encourage me through the tough days. I dutifully countered the first offer, but I knew in my heart we were too far apart. I would rather keep operating the business and taking my money than short sell it. I wanted out but was far from desperate.

When I got a serious offer a couple of months later, negotiations started in earnest. I spoke with the potential buyer, Frank. He used to have a coconut water company with his brother. Now he was looking for something he could operate from home with his wife. The only part of the deal that gave me pause was that Patricia would also represent Frank as the buyer. I wasn't sure she could represent my best interest and his at the same time, but eventually I accepted this arrangement. I was assured it was common.

Frank and I exchanged a few rounds of counteroffers before we signed a deal sometime in mid-April. I was on Martha's Vineyard when the deal came through. Half of me was ecstatic. As for the other half, it was part admiration and part disbelief, and I was pretty sure there was an expression on my face that I would recognize. Best of all, the deal would close in May, so I would have time for some fun over the summer. Still, I had six weeks of due diligence ahead of me, and it seemed like a long way to closure.

On my side, due diligence was simple. I just needed to know he was good for the money he was offering, which bank letters and escrow satisfied. Frank's side was a lot more complicated. He wanted details on nearly every line of my profit/loss sheet. My accountant told me how to generate reports and then export them into a spreadsheet, where I could reorganize the data and take out customer or vendor names. Daily I would find new demands for one report or another, orders, revenue or expenses sliced and diced this way and that. As the six-week deadline came due, Frank said he didn't have the loan finalized and requested that we extend for three more weeks. I agreed and we continued to work to meet each other's needs.

As the process went on, I needed to treat Frank like a prospective boss. If his demands felt unreasonable to me, it was not my job to judge him but to satisfy his needs. It was a difficult transition and there were a lot of demands by Frank and his bank as they worked out the loan. Three weeks later, he requested another extension.

At the same time, orders were increasing. Big orders and small orders, reorders and new orders—everyone seemed to want bags all of a sudden. As June moved into July, I was essentially working two jobs, running my bag business and selling it.

When Frank asked me to extend the closing date a fourth time, I balked. It was mid-July, months after the original closing date. I had a few containers getting ready to ship amounting to over a quarter-million bags. What if I was ruining my summer, working two jobs, and he never got to the finish line? I started to feel worn down and maybe taken in. I called my lawyer. Did I have to sign this latest extension?

Plain and simple, he said, no. I could throw the whole deal by not signing the extension unless Frank could come up with the money that week.

I reached out to Patricia and let her know I had lost faith in the deal and would not be signing the extension. I let her know that I had done everything I could, and if he didn't want to hit the date we agreed to, business was good, and I was happy reaping the profits myself.

That caused a flurry of emails and phone calls. Frank had sunk a lot of time and money into this deal. I told them that wasn't my concern. Things went blissfully quiet for a few days and then, I got a call from Patricia's boss, the owner of the business brokerage. He tried to be nice, but he explained that there was an arbitration clause in the contract, so if Frank wanted to invoke it—and I was assured he would—I would have to come back to Los Angeles for arbitration and hire counsel. It was a threat. I let him know I might take my chances. Frank was the one who couldn't stick to deadlines and complete his end of the deal. There wasn't much to arbitrate that I could see. Then he said I should think about what I needed to come back to the table. Those were the words I wanted to hear.

I spent a day or two thinking what would compensate me for the delays. The money I was generating was good and getting better. But I still didn't want to run the business. I didn't want to face more years of that kind of loneliness, and if I pulled out now, it would be a while before I got another shot at selling. So, I sent an email to Patricia saying I would come back to the table if the deal included an additional $50,000 for the trouble I had been through. I also updated the inventory valuation and told her how much it would cost them to buy me out if we signed the extension to August fourth. By then, I would have three containers either on the water or ready to ship. Inventory would push the price up another six figures at that date and I wanted Frank and his bankers to know. I was clear that if we didn't close on August fourth, the deal was done. Frank accepted.

The last week was a flurry of emails, mostly with me proving my inventory for Frank to submit to his bank, bills of lading, purchase orders, and estimates that would become invoices showing what customers would owe the company. Early on the morning of August fourth, I boarded a plane to Los Angeles. I got to LA and picked up Gary's car, which was parked at his offices. From west Los Angeles, I drove out to an escrow company in Rowland Heights, about 45 minutes east of downtown Los Angeles, out near Diamond Bar.

Weeks before, I imagined the closing, thinking it would be more official, something in a lawyer's offices. I bought a silk shirt for the occasion, not wanting to be outdressed in Los Angeles. A couple of days before closing, though, Patricia explained that the escrow company was on the second floor of a strip mall, and after we signed, we would leave and wait for the loan to come through.

Wait, I said. You mean we could sign the papers and the loan still might not come through?

There's always a possibility, she said. You don't know what the bank will do until they do it.

I was assured that if it didn't come through, I would get the papers and company ownership back along with a down payment from Frank forfeiting his right to purchase the company. For sure, I wasn't going to dress up if there was still doubt, so I just went straight from the plane to the car to the strip mall in Rowland Heights. I'd been up since the wee hours and on a plane for six hours. The escrow offices weren't much to look at. I imagine, neither was I. Frank and I signed papers. It was about as unceremonious as it could be. We shook hands and left.

Had I just sold my company? Or not?

Back in the car, I wasn't sure. I would have to wait to see if the funds settled overnight. If they did, Gary told me to use his offices, so that Frank and I could begin transition. If not—I didn't even want to think about it. I had a thousand thoughts running through my mind as I drove through east LA, when suddenly a big yellow light appeared on the dashboard. *Oh no*, I thought. But the car was just warning me to get gas.

The next morning, there was a significant deposit in our bank account. Gary, three hours ahead of me on the East Coast, was the first to notice.

Holy cow! he texted me. Your deal funded!

I looked at the bank account and had never seen a number like that before. Gary ran big deals through his company, but this was mine. If Gary looked at funding me all those years before as an investment, he now could say he had returns many times over his original investment. The purchase price alone was more than 11 times my annual teaching salary all those years ago, not to mention that I'd been making three times my teacher's salary for nearly every year but one that I ran the business. Certainly, I'd had a bad year with SnapSac, and without that, the number would have been even bigger.

Still, looking back, I wouldn't have changed anything. For someone who was never expected to make any money, I had just earned a lot of face and a seat at the table. If running my own business was like getting an emergency MBA every day, I just graduated.

Throughout my time running 1 Bag at a Time, I tried unsuccessfully to get store owners to require that the question at checkout change from *Paper or plastic?* to *Would you like a bag?* Over the last decade or so, it seems to have changed by itself. More than any other metric, I measure my impact by the number of cashiers who, by changing the question they ask their customers, continue to change consumer behavior and culture every day.

# Chapter 14

# Eight Principles that Helped
# Me Beat the Odds

If there's one thing I learned during my time as an entrepreneur, it's the power of changing the question in order to change everything else. Not long after I sold my company, I realized that the question I'd been asking myself—was I a good boss?— was the wrong question. That question, too, had to change. About a week before the sale went through, I went to lunch at a friend's house in Martha's Vineyard. The host, David, is a hugely successful venture capitalist, with a ton of energy, really smart, and intuitive about other people. His wife is one of my best friends and was part of my book group for years. In the middle of lunch, David saw I was in a bit of a fog, so he came over and sat next to me.

Do you know what you want to do when you sell your company, he asked?

Thinking about what I would do next overwhelmed and scared me. No, I admitted with a smile.

I'll tell you what you want to do, he continued. You want to be a business coach and you're going to be very good at it.

I'd never heard of coaching and asked him what it was about.

I have a coach, he said, and it's the best part of my week. My coach is always in my corner. I can tell him anything that's going on and he walks me through my thoughts on it. Look, everyone makes mistakes in business, but my coach helps me think about the things that are hard to think about. I make fewer mistakes because of him. You are going to be great at it.

My mind immediately flashed back to SnapSac, not my only mistake, but my worst. I thought how it might have been different if I'd had a weekly call with someone that I trusted who could make a case for me to slow down, or who might have suggested that sales deals were normally based on commission. In hindsight, I recognized how valuable it would have been to have a business coach.

A few weeks later, after the deal went through, I started investigating coaching, what it meant, what it takes to become one. Of course, I was happy with what I'd accomplished, thrilled really. Still, I was convinced that if I'd had a coach, I would have done even better. Maybe a lot better.

As I learned about coaching, I began to see that it would bring together everything I knew, the Socratic method I learned in my teaching career, the business knowledge I acquired over the last decade as an entrepreneur, and my love of working and connecting with people. David was right—I did want to become a business coach.

As I embarked on coach training, I returned to the questions that I still had not answered. Before long, I realized that it was not about being a good boss or a bad boss. The problem was that I saw myself as a boss, a person in charge who makes decisions.

I realized that seeing myself as an authority figure prevented me from seeing myself as a leader. A leader, as I was to learn, is a person who provides an inspiring vision for a talented team of people who want to grow and contribute to a growing organization and stretch what it can do. Companies that succeed exceptionally are built by teams where everyone has the opportunity to take on new challenges, develop new skills, and try ideas that make the whole better in a way that one person alone can't do.

A boss spends a lot of time telling people what they are expected to do. However, a leader spends time creating a vision for success and challenging the team with new experiences, mentoring them, supporting them when they fail, and helping them try again smarter and better next time. Leaders outperform bosses.

Looking back, I saw that actually, I had been a good leader for my production and logistics teams. Amy and the factory owners who helped produce my product all performed highly for me, and many stretched, learned, and became better at what they did, ultimately making my company better. From the start, I knew none of them worked for me directly and that they didn't have to do what I needed them to do. I knew that in order to get what I needed, I would have to make them want to come up to my standards. My best option was to inspire them to do better and stretch. When they caught my excitement, they did.

I did the same for a lot of my clients. I inspired hundreds of retailers to change their business model and stop hiding the cost of cheap bags from consumers, instead charging consumers directly for an affordable bag. I never got any one of them to change the question at checkout, but I convinced a lot of them to make reusable bags visible at the checkout stand, where customers need them most, and to promote bags in various ways. For many customers, I offered new products and helped them grow bag offerings over the years as consumer desires evolved.

I didn't turn those talents on for my team in LA because, well, I was their boss. They had to work for me. It turns out, when you have to do something, you don't put much heart or effort into doing it. You just do what you have to do. But when you want to do your job, when you're inspired to stretch, grow, and reach for higher goals, you start overperforming. That's why leaders outperform bosses. Leaders spend their days focused on helping people love their job and grow. As a coach, I would dedicate myself to a mission of helping people become better leaders.

My heart still swells when I recognize that I was a good entrepreneur, good enough to start up a company, handle a hockey-stick curve, accomplish a mission, survive my worst mistakes, and complete the business cycle through to sale. That in itself is a huge win, and I learned a lot along the way.

Believing in myself and being driven by a mission greater than myself gave me the energy to keep going even through the longest days and darkest nights. If I had been motivated by money, I would have failed. What kept me going was my dedication to a purpose and to other people—the people along my supply chain and the consumers who adopted my bags. I couldn't let them down. Because it was never about me, I always found the energy to keep going.

As I look back, I think the most courageous action I took was not the first money I wired to China or quitting my job, but simply letting go of what other people thought about me. I let myself dream and be inspired by a vision that, at first, only I could imagine. Certainly, it scared me a little bit, but I have learned, that is what a good dream should do. If it started as a spark, I nurtured the flame until I felt a burning passion and moral imperative to make the world better. For the next ten years, I fed that fire until my passion carried me far beyond where anyone else would have thought.

Ultimately, my mission ended up changing me. Although I learned a lot, what helped me succeed was not so much the knowledge or lessons I learned, and more the principles that kept me on the right path even when I didn't know where I was going. I hope that the business principles I discovered will help you, too, beat the odds and succeed in achieving your wildest dreams.

Here are the eight principles that helped me beat the odds:

1. If you're going to be something, be the best. Don't let other people's expectations hold you back.
2. Write a mission that lights a fire in your heart and pursue it every day. Resist the temptation to drift into new activities that don't contribute directly to your mission.
3. Balance what you feel with what you know. What you feel, and what others around you feel, will motivate

and drive your actions. Use science and data as a reality check and make sure you are on the right path before you commit. By honoring the feelings of those around you and balancing your decisions with real knowledge, you will make better decisions.

4. Write a story that will convey your passion. Tell everyone your story and improve it as you find out what resonates with people. Use it to connect emotionally with others before getting down to business.

5. Dedicate yourself to respect for all people and the planet. When you demonstrate your respect for people and the planet, by your daily interactions and by the occasional hard decisions that make your commitment manifest, you will earn the respect of others and begin to truly lead them.

6. Track your cash flow carefully and try to match your projections. If you miss your targets, figure out why, adjust, and try again. If you hit them, set higher targets. Be bold in your projections.

7. Keep your promises to customers, vendors, and employees. Take responsibility when things go wrong. Build relationships of trust.

8. Be a leader, not a boss. Spend most of your time inspiring everyone to believe in your mission and vision for success. Hire people you respect and expect them to learn, grow, and contribute new ideas to improve your results. Invest in others and encourage them to take on projects that stretch their skills. Give them goals that make them reach and support them as they overcome challenges. Recognize and reward success. Ask what they are learning often.

Your mission doesn't have to be anything extraordinary. Honestly, grocery bags are pretty unremarkable as a dream or purpose in life. What happened when I focused on just this one thing was surprising.

All you need to start making a difference in your world is a belief in the value of what you want to do. Sure, success will take a lot of hard work, but the only way to fail is to quit. If you just keep going, you can do anything. Maybe, like me, if you just do one thing, you too can put a wedge in the whole works and have an outsized impact. That's how you change the world, one mission at a time.

## Epilogue

# I'd Love to Hear from You

If you are inspired by my story, let me know the problems that light a fire in your heart. You don't have to know how to solve them. You just need to believe in yourself and your ability to make a difference.

I'm happy to answer your questions, cheer you on, and offer support as, together, we make the world a better place.

You can find me through my website:

https://lisadfostercoach.com

## About the Author

# Lisa D. Foster, Ph.D., ACC, CPRW

Lisa D. Foster is a business coach whose mission is to help managers become better leaders by using emotional intelligence to create the conditions for high performance. In 2005, she founded 1 Bag at a Time, Inc., a first-to-market reusable grocery bag company. As a former high-school English teacher and purpose-driven eco-entrepreneur, she became a pioneer in the fight against single-use plastic, and her company ranked in the top three bag suppliers in the US during her leadership. Currently, Lisa serves on the Board at Sheriff's Meadow Foundation and as a Corporator Emeritus at Northeastern University, Boston.

https://lisadfostercoach.com

# Notes

## Introduction

1. To learn more about how business is changing now, I highly recommend Harvard Business Professor Rosabeth Moss Kanter's book, *Think Outside the Building* (2020, PublicAffairs, New York), detailing how advanced leadership can create public and private partnerships like The Global Ocean Trust (http://globaloceantrust.com/en/) to address complex environmental problems. I also recommend Harvard Business Professor Rebecca Henderson's book, *Reimagining Capitalism in a World on Fire* (2020, PublicAffairs, New York), which details at length the many businesses that have already changed their business models to improve outcomes for people and the planet.

## Chapter 1

2. LA County Supervisors Staff Report. 2007. *An Overview of Carryout Bags in Los Angeles County*. PDF. https://ladpw. org/epd/pdf/PlasticBagReport.pdf. Page 2. Government report.
3. Ellen MacArthur Foundation. 2016. *The New Plastic Economy*. PDF. https://www.ellenmacarthurfoundation.org/assets/ downloads/publications/NPEC-Hybrid_English_22-11-17_ Digital.pdf. Executive Summary. PDF. Nonprofit report.
4. Jun. 5, 2019. *The Great Pacific Garbage Patch*. National Geographic Encyclopedia. Webpage. https://www.national geographic.org/encyclopedia/great-pacific-garbage-patch/. Magazine article.
5. Ellen MacArthur Foundation. 2016. *The New Plastic Economy*. PDF. https://www.ellenmacarthurfoundation. org/assets/downloads/publications/NPEC-Hybrid_English _22-11-17_Digital.pdf. Executive Summary. PDF. Nonprofit

report.

6. Ellen MacArthur Foundation. 2016. *The New Plastic Economy.* PDF. https://www.ellenmacarthurfoundation.org/assets/ downloads/publications/NPEC-Hybrid_English_22-11-17_ Digital.pdf. Executive Summary. Nonprofit report.

7. *The New Plastics Economy: Rethinking the Future of Plastics.* Jan. 2016. World Economic Forum. https://www3.weforum. org/docs/WEF_The_New_Plastics_Economy.pdf. PDF. Nonprofit report.

8. Chris Jordan. Photographic Arts. 2009 to unknown dates. *Midway: Message from the Gyre 2009–Present.* http://www. chrisjordan.com/gallery/midway/#CF000313%2018x24. Webpage.

9. *Ocean Plastics Pollution: A Global Tragedy for Our Oceans and Sea Life.* Center for Biological Diversity. Accessed Dec. 1, 2021. https://www.biologicaldiversity.org/campaigns/ ocean_plastics/. Webpage.

10. Fiona Harvey. Feb. 26, 2019. *Plastics Leading to Reproductive Problems for Wildlife.* The Guardian. https://www.theguardi an.com/environment/2019/feb/27/plastics-leading-to-repro ductive-problems-for-wildlife. News article.

11. Marla Cone. Jun. 19, 2003. *Of Polar Bears and Pollution.* Los Angeles Times. https://www.latimes.com/archives/la-xpm-2003-jun-19-me-polarbears19-story.html. News article.

12. Alisa L. Rich, Laura M. Phipps, Sweta Tiwari, Hemanth Rudraraju, Phillip O. Dokpesi. Sep. 8, 2016. Environmental Health Insights. *The Increasing Prevalence in Intersex Variation from Toxicological Dysregulation in Fetal Reproductive Tissue Differentiation and Development by Endocrine-Disrupting Chemicals.* National Institute of Health. https://www.ncbi. nlm.nih.gov/pmc/articles/PMC5017538/. Journal article abstract.

13. Shanna H. Swan and Colino Stacey. Feb. 23, 2021. *Count Down: How Our Modern World Is Threatening Sperm Counts,*

*Altering Male and Female Reproductive Development, and Imperiling the Future of the Human Race* (Scribner, New York). Book. See also Shanna Swan and Stacey Colino, Mar. 16, 2021, *Reproductive Problems in Both Men and Women Are Rising at an Alarming Rate*. Scientific American, online. https://www.scientificamerican.com/article/reproductive-problems-in-both-men-and-women-are-rising-at-an-alarming-rate/. News article online.

## Chapter 2

14. Nolan ITU, Pty Ltd. Dec. 2002. *Plastic Shopping Bags—Analysis of Levies and Environmental Impacts Final Report*. Australian Department of the Environment and Heritage. https://www.environment.gov.au/archive/settlements/publications/waste/plastic-bags/analysis.html. PDF. Government report.

## Chapter 3

15. Treacy Hogan. Aug. 20, 1999. *Green Tax on Shoppers to Put £40m on Bills*. The Independent. https://www.independent.ie/irish-news/green-tax-on-shoppers-to-put-40m-on-bills-26141639.html. News article.

16. Mark Brennock. Aug. 20, 1999. *Minister Preparing to Put Tax on Plastic Bags*. The Irish Times. https://www.irishtimes.com/news/minister-preparing-to-put-tax-on-plastic-bags-1.218311. News article.

17. Mark Brennock. Aug. 21, 2001. *Plastic Bag Levy Succeeds Spectacularly*. The Irish Times. https://www.irishtimes.com/news/plastic-bag-levy-succeeds-spectacularly-1.1092623. News article.

18. Kat Kerlin. Sep. 24, 2015. *Plastic for Dinner: A Quarter of Fish Sold at Markets Contain Human-Made Debris*. UC Davis News. https://www.ucdavis.edu/news/plastic-dinner-quarter-fish-sold-markets-contain-human-made-debris/. University study, news article.

19. Alexandra McInturf and Matthew Savoca. Feb. 15, 2021. *The Fish We Eat Are Eating Plastic.* The Maritime Executive. https://www.maritime-executive.com/editorials/the-fish-we-eat-are-eating-plastic. News article on study with ecologist Elliott Hazen.

20. Shanna H. Swan and Colino Stacey. Feb. 23, 2021. *Count Down: How Our Modern World Is Threatening Sperm Counts, Altering Male and Female Reproductive Development, and Imperiling the Future of the Human Race* (Scribner, New York). Book.

## Chapter 5

21. Marcia Anderson. Nov. 1, 2016. *Confronting Plastic Pollution One Bag at a Time.* EPA blog. https://blog.epa.gov/2016/11/01/confronting-plastic-pollution-one-bag-at-a-time/. Blog.

## Chapter 6

22. Kitt Doucette. Jul. 25, 2011. *The Plastic Bag Wars.* The Rolling Stone. https://www.rollingstone.com/politics/politics-news/the-plastic-bag-wars-243547/. Magazine article.

## Chapter 8

23. LA County Supervisors Staff Report. 2007. *An Overview of Carryout Bags in Los Angeles County.* PDF. https://ladpw.org/epd/pdf/PlasticBagReport.pdf. Page 2, 3. Government report.

24. LA County Supervisors Staff Report. 2007. *An Overview of Carryout Bags in Los Angeles County.* PDF. https://ladpw.org/epd/pdf/PlasticBagReport.pdf. Page 4. Government report.

## Chapter 11

25. Scott Harrison. Sep. 30, 2010. *Rise Above Plastics.* http://riseaboveplastics.blogspot.com/2010/09/. Blog post.

26. Cole Rosengren. Nov. 9, 2017. *Cleanup Crews Report Litter*

*Reduction One Year after California Passes Bag Ban.* Waste Dive. https://www.wastedive.com/news/cleanup-crews-report-litter-reduction-one-year-after-california-passes-bag/510504/. Blog.

## Chapter 12

27. My research in 2016 found studies showing 60% of consumers using reusable bags most of the time when they shopped. While those studies are no longer available, I use this number as an estimate. A nationwide survey my company conducted in 2011 found 54% of Americans used reusable bags most of the time when they shopped, long before the New York and California bag bans. Now, according to government surveys, in many localities, the number is higher, for example 65.9% in Charlotte, NC *(https://www.charleston-sc.gov/DocumentCenter/ View/14402/Survey-Report-for-City-of-CHS-website?bidId=);* 90% in Decatur, GA *(find link at https://www.decaturga.com/ bc-esb);* and in some places somewhat lower, for example, 42% in Tacoma, WA *(https://cms.cityoftacoma.org/Sustainability/ Public_Bag_Survey_Summarized_Results.pdf).* In California *(https://www.surfrider.org/coastal-blog/entry/why-bag-laws-work-study-shows-californias-statewide-bill-a-success),* reusable bags are used in 86% of transactions.

# References and Links to Further Reading

## Reports

The Australian Department of the Environment and Heritage. *Plastic Shopping Bags—Analysis of Levies and Environmental Impacts Final Report.*

Ellen MacArthur Foundation. 2016. *The New Plastic Economy.* PDF. https://www.ellenmacarthurfoundation.org/assets/downloads/publications/NPEC-Hybrid_English_22-11-17_Digital.pdf.

LA County Supervisors Staff Report. 2007. *An Overview of Carryout Bags in Los Angeles County.* PDF. https://ladpw.org/epd/pdf/PlasticBagReport.pdf.

## Books

Malcolm Gladwell. Feb. 2000. *The Tipping Point: How Little Things Can Make a Big Difference* (Little Brown, New York).

Rebecca Henderson. Apr. 2020. *Reimagining Capitalism in a World on Fire* (PublicAffairs, New York). https://reimaginingcapitalism. org/

Professor Rosabeth Moss Kanter. 2020. *Think Outside the Building* (PublicAffairs, New York). https://www.publicaffairsbooks.com/titles/rosabeth-moss-kanter/think-outside-the-building/9781541742727/

Shanna H. Swan and Colino Stacey. Feb. 23, 2021. *Count Down: How Our Modern World Is Threatening Sperm Counts, Altering Male and Female Reproductive Development, and Imperiling the Future of the Human Race* (Scribner, New York). https://www.simonandschuster.com/books/Count-Down/Shanna-H-Swan/9781982113667

CHANGEMAKERS
BOOKS

Transform your life, transform *our* world. Changemakers
Books publishes books for people who seek to become positive,
powerful agents of change. These books inform, inspire, and
provide practical wisdom and skills to empower us to write
the next chapter of humanity's future.
www.changemakers-books.com

# Current Bestsellers from Changemakers Books

## Goddess Luminary Leadership Wheel
*A Post-Patriarchal Paradigm*
Lynne Sedgmore
An exciting radical inclusive leadership development which transcends patriarchal and conventional limitations to liberate and transform you, and others, into Leaderful Luminaries.

## Integration
*The Power of Being Co-Active in Work and Life*
Karen Kimsey-House & Ann G Betz
Integration examines how we came to be polarized in our dealing with self and other, and what we can do to move from an either/or state to a more effective and fulfilling way of being.

## Resetting Our Future: What If Solving the Climate Crisis Is Simple?
Tom Bowman
Replacing gloomy global warming narratives with a simpler paradigm unearths new ways to empower action.

## Resetting Our Future: Learning from Tomorrow
*Using Strategic Foresight to Prepare for the Next Big Disruption*
Bart Édes
This book explains how Strategic Foresight can help organizations identify plausible alternative futures for their operational environment, and assist them in preparing for a range of eventualities.

**Resetting Our Future: Zero Waste Living, The 80/20 Way**
*The Busy Person's Guide to a Lighter Footprint*
Stephanie J. Miller
Empowering the busy individual to do the easy things that
have a real impact on the climate and waste crises.

**Resetting Our Future: SMART Futures
for a Flourishing World**
*A Paradigm Shift for Achieving Global Sustainability*
Claire A. Nelson
SMART futures is a 'systems literacy' approach to problem
solving that allows us to address challenges of our volatile,
uncertain, complex and ambiguous world as an integrated
whole

**Resetting Our Future: Impact ED
How Community College Entrepreneurship Creates
Equity and Prosperity**
Andrew Gold, Mary Beth Kerly & Rebecca A. Corbin
This book provides leaders with a roadmap to the future,
showing how entrepreneurial thinking and action can put
local communities on the path to recovery from the economic
devastation induced by the COVID-19 pandemic.